RUN TOWARDS THE LIGHT

A JOURNEY
INTO PURPOSE—PURSUING
A RELATIONSHIP OF PASSION,
COMMITMENT AND
SURRENDER TO JESUS

Charlie Roberts

RUN TOWARDS THE LIGHT

A JOURNEY INTO PURPOSE—PURSUING A RELATIONSHIP OF PASSION, COMMITMENT, AND SURRENDER TO JESUS

Charlie Roberts

In accordance with the U.S. Copyright Act of 2025, the scanning, uploading, and electronic sharing of any part of this book without the permission of the publisher or author is unlawful piracy and theft of intellectual property.

Copyright © 2025 Charlie Roberts, All rights reserved.

No part of this work may be reproduced; stored in a retrieval system, or transmitted in any form or means electronic, mechanical, photocopying, recording or otherwise, without the written prior permission of the authors, their assigns, or legal representatives.

The contents of this book include opinion, interpretation, and allegorical representation. Pixel Glyph Press, the author, and contributors to this work have made every effort to represent accurately the identity of real persons, places, or things mentioned. Predictions and promises in this book are based on the Word of God in the Bible, as given through various translations, experiences, and interpretations, including those of the author. No guarantees can be made for your personal experience, or how you will encounter the God of the Universe, except that you will and you must at some point encounter God.

Adult: Christian, Inspirational, Self-help
Paperback ISBN: 978-1-956579-97-0

Designed and Published by:

PIXEL GLYPH PRESS

PixelGlyphPress
Nolensville, Tennessee, 37135 USA

pixelglyphpress.com
Where authors find publishing support.
Pixel Glyph Press is an imprint of Daniel Rg Crandall Publisher.

All illustrations, biblical references, shared stories of recollection and personal experiences used in this book, are believed to be credited to the source and original author. Any similarities to other posts, illustrations and or stories are purely coincidental. Emphasis may have been added, or translations of scripture combined for the purposes of this book. The author has made, to the best of his ability, every effort to give credit, where credit is due.

THE HOLY BIBLE, NEW INTERNATIONAL VERSION® NIV®
Copyright © 1973, 1978, 1984 by International Bible Society®
Used by permission. All rights reserved worldwide.

The Holy Bible, New King James Version®. NKJV
Copyright © 1982 by Thomas Nelson, Inc. All rights reserved.

The Message is quoted: "Scripture taken from The Message. Copyright Â© 1993, 1994, 1995, 1996, 2000, 2001, 2002. Used by permission of NavPress Publishing Group."

Scripture taken from The Voice™. Copyright © 2012 by Ecclesia Bible Society. Used by permission. All rights reserved.

Scripture quotations marked "TLB" are taken from The Living Bible copyright © 1971. Used by permission of Tyndale House Publishers, a Division of Tyndale House Ministries, Carol Stream, Illinois 60188. All rights reserved.

Scriptures marked HCSB are taken from the HOLMAN CHRISTIAN STANDARD BIBLE (HCSB): Scripture taken from the HOLMAN CHRISTIAN STANDARD BIBLE, copyright© 1999, 2000, 2002, 2003 by Holman Bible Publishers, Nashville Tennessee. All rights reserved

"Scripture taken from the NEW AMERICAN STANDARD BIBLE®, Copyright © 1960, 1962, 1963, 1968, 1971, 1972, 1973, 1975, 1977, 1995 by The Lockman Foundation. Used by permission."

All Scripture marked with the designation "GW" is taken from GOD'S WORD®. © 1995, 2003, 2013, 2014, 2019, 2020 by God's Word to the Nations Mission Society. Used by permission.

Scripture quotations marked "TPT" are from The Passion Translation®. Copyright © 2017, 2018, 2020 by Passion & Fire Ministries, Inc. Used by permission. All rights reserved. ThePassionTranslation.com.

DEDICATIONS

To God the Father, Jesus my Lord and The Amazing Holy Spirit. I love You Guys and want to say thank you for the amazing relationship you have allowed me to have and be a part of! Thank You for Your never ending patience, love, grace and Your willingness to empower me, as well as forgive me. My life has never been the same, since the moment I met You! Each day I become more aware of Your love for myself, my family and all of mankind! I am humbled and honored to be part of your family, "the family of God"

To my wife Cindy, you are a continual inspiration to everyone who knows you, especially to me! Your laughter is so infectious and it continually brings joy to everyone and everywhere you go! I want to thank you for being who you are and for all you do. For helping with ideas and for being my sounding board and always offering an listening ear. Most of all, for your unconditional love and support! I never thought life could be so wonderful, until you became a part of it! Thank you for being my soulmate and my everything!

Kristin and Troy, thanks for all your help and taking your time to help edit this endeavor! I pray God blesses both your ministry and personal lives, richly!

To my church family and friends who might read and recognize something we may have talked about in this book. I would advise you, be careful with what you say, because I just might write it down. But seriously friends, I want to thank you for all your support and love, it means more than you'll ever know! Lastly, I would like to thank all those who God has directed to pour into me over the years! I know the number is great, but you all know who you are! I would also like to acknowledge all who have gone on to their reward! I would like to thank you for all your continued prayers. And I want you to know God is still answering them, so keep them up as we all continue to "Run Towards The Light!"

FOREWORD

Every author who has written anything, would hope what they have written would help their reader, myself included. I hope what God has inspired me to write will make a difference in your relationship with Jesus and in your spiritual life! Not because of my involvement, but because of my willingness to say yes and to listen to the leading of the Spirit of God.

Some of the things contained in this book, may seem to be new to you. While the truth is, most of what you will read you may have heard before, or already know. These well known principles and ideas, which God gave us, work flawlessly in our lives. But probably we haven't been doing, or may have never done them consistently in our walk with the Lord!

Why do we find it difficult to do what we know is the correct thing to do? Truthfully, I think if we would all be faithful to our calling and do the basics of what Jesus told us to do, we could turn the world upside down, just as the disciples did in their day! Lord knows we need to, as we march ever so close to the end of the age and the return of our Lord Jesus.

I could make several promises concerning this book and the content of it, but a promise on my part, without a commitment on your part, would only deliver an empty result. What I can say is: I promise what is in this book will change your life, if you make a commitment to implement and practice what you find and if you always,...

RUN TOWARDS THE LIGHT!

BACK COVER:

RUN TOWARDS THE LIGHT explores humanity's connection to the divine and the true pursuit of authentic purpose and calling. The book unveils the unique destination and divine assignment for every individual person.

Join us on this journey of exploration, self-discovery, and transformation as we uncover what God has in store for us all. Let's strive to fulfill the coveted words, "Well done, good and faithful servant," as we collectively move forward.

I promise that the messages in this book will change your life, if you make a commitment to implement and practice what you learn, and if you always, *RUN TOWARDS THE LIGHT!*

RUN TOWARDS THE LIGHT

CHAPTER 1
IT'S NOT WHERE YOU'VE BEEN—IT'S *WHERE YOU'RE GOING*   8

CHAPTER 2
JUST WAITING FOR YOU   17

CHAPTER 3
IT'S NOT OVER YOUR HEAD—IT'S UNDER YOUR FEET.   28

CHAPTER 4
THE POWERFUL VOICE OF UNITY   36

CHAPTER 5
SOME PLANT, SOME WATER—WHICH ONE ARE YOU?   50

CHAPTER 6
IS GOD'S PLAN, YOUR PLAN?   66

CHAPTER 7
RECEIVE YOUR CALLING   77

CHAPTER 8
WHAT DOES A MOVE OF GOD LOOK LIKE?   86

CHAPTER 9
WHEN WILL ENOUGH BE ENOUGH?   96

CHAPTER 10
PUT ME IN COACH   106

CHAPTER 11
HURRY UP, HAVE FAITH AND WAIT   116

CHAPTER 12
NOTHING ELSE MATTERS   127

CHAPTER 13
YOU CAN BE FREE   136

CHAPTER 14
ACCOUNTABILITY STARTS TODAY   145

CHAPTER 1

IT'S NOT WHERE YOU'VE BEEN—IT'S *WHERE YOU'RE GOING*

In the North Sea, at Firth of Tay, Scotland, there is a dangerous rock to navigators. Every tide that comes in covers the rock just beneath the surface of the waters. Many ships have been damaged by this hidden rock.

The *Abbot of Aberbrothok* fixed a great warning bell and attached it to the rock. For several years, the ringing of the bell was a sound of warning to all ships passing. Not one ship was damaged during this time.

Then one day, a sea pirate stole the bell, and sold it for a good profit. Twelve months later, the pirate who stole the bell, while on a speedy mission sailing through the same area, crashed his vessel. Both he and his crew perished in the icy cold waters of the North Sea. [SOURCE: bellrock.org.uk]

His crew followed his direction and asked no questions, trusting his ability to navigate. Many have done so throughout history. All the way from Genesis to Revelation, from one disastrous situation to another! Here's a novel idea. Before we ever let others lead us anywhere, wouldn't it be helpful to know if they knew where their so called sense of direction and leadership might end up leading you too!

There are far too many people just existing in the world. By most standards, they're not really living; just trying to find any sense of purpose. Blindly trusting those who claim to have the answers. **They are following people who have no idea where they are going, or leading**

them to. Only interested in being in the popular crowd or jumping on the next big craze. And one day, they wake up like the crew of the sneaky pirate. Discovering it's too late!

So many people feel as though they're stuck in their life, going nowhere! Completely oblivious to the fact that the journey they're on, should be leading them to a life of true worth and value. But it's not. **They are too distracted trying to fit in with the world, forgetting the best part about life is the journey to the destination they're heading to!** And the reason they feel stuck is that they have no calling on their life, or clear sense of direction!

Like it or not, believe it or not, we are all headed somewhere, whether we want to admit it or not. And while you may not realize it, or want to hear it, the destination is either an endless heaven or an endless hell! And ultimately, we are the ones responsible for choosing which path we take. **Every decision, every action, for better or worse, shapes our journey.** A cold sobering fact of reality, far too many have yet come to believe or accept.

Many days have passed, so many situations have come and gone on my own journey. So many great people I've come to know along the way! There were some players with small bit parts, and I couldn't wait to see them exit. And others with great influence, playing major roles in the script of my life. I still remember and miss them deeply. However, one truth stands high above all others. **God has never let me down; not once!**

There were times when it felt like the world was against me, when the darkness seemed so overwhelming. But I always held on to my faith and by the grace of God, somehow found the strength to pursue the light of God's love, rather than the temptations and pitfalls of the world!

Sometimes I easily said the words, "I'm not going to participate" and other times with tears in my eyes, hanging on to scripture claiming, "greater is He who is in me than He who is in the world!" **And still other times I've said thankfully, "There go I, but by the grace of God".**

Jesus has always been right by my side, along with the Holy Spirit living in me, walking with me, speaking to me, directing my steps and pouring into me. I think I could accurately confide, friend, that probably more times than I could ever imagine, Jesus faithfully carried me across the finish line.

How about you? Is your story similar? **We all have a story to tell! That's your testimony! Have you been carried many times across the finish line? Or are you still lost?** Are you aimlessly wandering and looking for help, waiting for a sign to guide you in the right direction?

I can tell you I have been there, feeling lost and unsure, with each step I took. Weighed down by doubt and uncertainty, more times than I can remember! But every time I actually listened, used my God given faith and started to run towards the light, instead of from it, the light got amazingly brighter with each step! I always felt closer to God every time! But in reality I'm pretty sure, each time, I realized how much closer Jesus always was to me than I realized!

The best instruction manual ever written, says in Proverbs 3:5 that you can *Trust in the Lord with all your heart, and lean not on your own understanding; In all your ways acknowledge Him, and He shall direct your paths.*

One of the most difficult things to do in any single given situation, is to relinquish our control and or ability, to make our own choices. To totally depend on someone else to lead and guide you, into a life they claim is going to be great!

Most people don't have a problem giving up trust/control in any given situation, once they realize they've reached their wit's end, and there's no hope! But to give up all control and let someone else lead you, your whole life through, is a different story. Sadly, keeping a lot of people from living the amazing life God has always had prepared for them! The reality is, far too many people don't know the difference, even when they have witnessed the event.

God's idea of life is different by all standards and definitions! Why? Because God's idea of life is life on the grand scale. The Bible calls it "abundant life" with the parameters set by God's supernatural capabilities, instead of man's limited ones!

Romans 8:31 MSG —*So, what do you think? With God on our side like this, how can we lose? If God didn't hesitate to put everything on the line for us, embracing our condition and exposing himself to the worst by sending his own Son, is there anything else he wouldn't gladly and freely do for us? And who would dare tangle with God by messing with one of God's chosen? Who would dare even to point a finger? None of this fazes us because Jesus loves us. I'm absolutely convinced that nothing—nothing living or dead, angelic or demonic, today or tomorrow, high or low, thinkable or unthinkable—absolutely nothing can get between us and God's love because of the way that Jesus our Master has embraced us.*

I love what Jesus' words declare in Luke chapter seven [The Passion translation]: **"The blessing of heaven comes upon those who never lose their faith in me, no matter what happens."**

Never lose Jesus' blessing, as long as you never lose your faith in Him! I love this word. It means, as long as you **Run Towards the Light of Jesus, seek Him and walk in relationship with Jesus, His blessings (got to love this promise) will never stop pursuing you!**

Follow the light of Jesus, or follow the darkness of Satan? Wow… this certainly seems like it would be the biggest no-brainer of all time!

But, I have to ask something personal. How much do you want out of this life you have been given? Followed up with another question: How much do you want to pursue, trust and receive of God?

Because the second question will always determine the first one each and everyday, your whole life through!

My friends, no matter what happens in the world and in this life that we are living, we should never stop the pursuit of our relationship and trust in God's ability to meet our every need, no matter what it is!

Not so many years ago, there was a song called "what the world needs now is love, sweet love" and it went on to say, "It's the one thing that there's just too little of!" I want you to understand how much Jesus really loves you! Because the realization makes it so much easier to trust Him and wait on His direction in your life!

When you finally realize for yourself, down in the depths of your spirit, how amazing God's grace really is, the revelation is life-changing! Life-changing! There are a lot of people, both good and bad, who will come into your life and act like they care about you, but no one will ever care for you like Jesus!

Hymnast, Charles Weigle wrote these life changing words, almost one hundred years ago in 1932:

> *No one ever cared for me like Jesus;*
> *There's no other friend so kind as He.*
> *No one else could take the sin and darkness from me;*
> *O how much He cared for me.*

More recently, *Elevation Worship* sings these life-changing words:

> *I'm calling on the God of Jacob,*
> *Whose love endures through generations,*
> *I know that You will keep Your covenant....*
> *O God, my God, I need You.*
> *O God, my God, I need You now, How I need You now.*

The God who took care of Jacob, Moses, and Charles Weigle, just 100 years ago, is the very same God who longs for and desires to love you and take care of you, everyday of your life.

> Jeremiah 29:11-13 THE VOICE — *For I know the plans I have for you," says the Eternal, "plans for peace, not evil, to give you a future and hope—never forget that. At that time, you will call out for Me, and I will hear. You will pray, and I will listen. You will look for Me intently, and you will find Me.*

Remember the two questions I asked earlier? How much do you want out of life? Also followed up with another question. How much do you want to pursue, trust and receive from God? Again I ask, because this can't be stressed enough! The second question always determines the first one each and every day, your whole life through!

No matter what happens in the world, no matter what happens in this life we are living, we should give our highest priority to Him, above all else. Never stop the pursuit of a relationship with Him. And trusting God's ability to meet our every need, no matter what it is!

If we want to experience and embrace the plans God has for us, we have to and must, run towards the light of the world. His name is Jesus! God has the ability to deliver what He says He can do, knows how to deliver and wants to deliver for us, when we pursue and acknowledge who His Son Jesus is!

1 Peter 5:7 says: "cast," —which means to throw, "—your cares, anxieties and worries on Him, because He cares about you."

Listen friend, if we're ever going to get out from under the weight of our own issues and the world inflicted issues we face every day, **we need to get in the continual habit of giving everything we face and everyone we know to Jesus.** We need to daily let go, keep our heads up and walk towards the light. In layman's terms, we need to release—say it with me, "release, release, release,"—not want or ask for them back. Let them become His problems and only His!

Did you know, Jesus has no problems? That's right. **Jesus has no problems,** seriously! Even the problems you have, that you think are unsolvable and have been giving to Him and taking back, over and over again.

I'll tell you what Jesus has plenty of: Solutions! That's right. **Jesus has solutions, and more solutions on top of those solutions!**

Jesus has your answer and solution to your every problem, because **Jesus has already defeated and been victorious over every problem imaginable—even yours!**

You may not believe me or want to believe this truth could even be a possibility. What concerns you concerns God. What concerns you, concerns Jesus! Think about it this way, do you think somebody who was willing to die for your salvation, would stop His concern for you at the dying part?

The answer is *No, infinitely no!* Jesus not only died for you, but He rose from the grave victorious over sin and death. He rose victoriously so you could live a victorious, abundant life! A better life than you could ever deserve, or dream!

So whenever you're faced with problems, situations and obstacles that seem insurmountable, throw them on Jesus! Release them and rest assured in the "more than enough faith" God has given you! Jesus can handle all your concerns!

Your part is only to believe; **in case you haven't figured out what your part is in all of this. It's to believe** and accept that Jesus willingly wants to do what you ask of Him!

I love the way the next two passages of scripture read:

> 1 Cor. 1:9 MSG — *God, who got you started in this spiritual adventure, shares with us the life of his Son and our Master Jesus. He will never give up on you. Never forget that.*

God is 100% faithful! Our faithfulness is not part of His faithfulness! That means God's 100% faithfulness is not dependent on anything we do! Aren't you glad that's the way it is? I know I am! I believe if God's way of thinking were a self-help book, it would be called "a relationship guide for dummies!"

> 2 Timothy 2:13 NKJV — *If we are faithless, He remains faithful; He cannot deny Himself.*

The way God thinks towards you and me, is what makes the lyrics to the song "Same God" so relevant that I shared earlier with you! "I'm calling on the God of Jacob, Whose love endures through generations, I know that You will keep Your covenant."

Let me remind you, just in case you get lost in the struggle of your need at any given moment! Because, I know firsthand... It is so easy to get lost in the middle of the struggle! It is so easy to get lost when it's your mountain of need on the prayer request table and not someone else's!

Think about this, and get ready to wrap your arms around this next statement, and don't ever let go of who you are and what is possible in its context! The same God, **the VERY SAME GOD, that delivered Samson, David, Jacob, Moses, Ruth, Esther, Noah, and Abraham! The VERY SAME**

GOD is willing and wants to deliver you, from every need you will ever have!

JESUS, will never (as you're reading this RIGHT NOW, say "Never, Never... Never, Never, Never!") Jesus will *never* leave you or forsake you. Jesus is a friend that sticks closer than a brother. God's word declares, Jesus never changes His position or his line of thinking either.

> Hebrews 13:8 NKJV *Jesus Christ is the same yesterday, today, and forever.*

Jesus has a proven track record; why not let His plans become your plans? Jesus has complete access to the very best plans to prosper you and give you hope and to keep you from harm! If you haven't made Him The Lord of your Life, right now in this very moment, would be a good time to start letting Him lead, guide and direct your life.

I'm not only talking about making Jesus the Saviour of your life...I'm talking about an ***all-in commitment of surrender, making the decision to always Run Towards the Light, no matter what happens!***

Dr. James Dobson told the story, *No Lights on the Runway*:

> *Consider the experience of a friend of mine, who was a recreational pilot, when he was younger. On one occasion, he flew his single-engine plane toward his home base at a small, country airport.*
>
> *Unfortunately, he waited too long to start back and arrived in the vicinity of the field as the sun dropped behind a mountain. By the time he maneuvered his plane into position to land, he could not see the hazy runway below.*
>
> *There were no lights to guide him and no one on duty at the airport. He circled the field for another attempt to land, but by then the darkness had become even more impenetrable. For two desperate hours, he flew his plane around and around in the blackness of the night, knowing that probably death awaited him when he ran out of fuel. Then as greater panic gripped him, a miracle occurred.*

Someone on the ground heard the continuing drone of his engine and realized his predicament. That merciful man drove his car back and forth on the runway to show my friend the location of the airstrip. Then he let his lights cast their beam from the far end while the plane landed.

How many of us have been in the hovering mode of life far too long? Even though friends and family have been running their vehicles up and down life's runway, trying to show us the way, the whole time.

It's not where you've been that matters, it's where you're going! And if you will keep your focus and Run Towards the Light, there's no place that you can't go. **Where you are going, God is ready and willing to take you!**

CHAPTER 2

JUST WAITING FOR YOU

I heard the story of a family who was on vacation at the lake one summer. Dad had been puttering out by the boat house. Two of his sons, a 12-year old and a 3-year old, were down playing along the dock. The 12-year old was supposed to be watching his little brother, but he got distracted. The 3-year old, little Billy, thought that would be a good time to check out the shiny aluminum fishing boat tied up at the end of the dock. So he went to the dock and put one foot on the boat and one foot on the dock. He lost his balance and fell into the water, which was about 5 or 6 feet deep.

The splash alerted the 12-year old who let out a piercing scream. Dad came running from the boat house, jumped into the water, swam down, but unable to see anything, came up for air. Sick with panic, he went right back down into this murky water and began to feel everywhere around the bottom. He couldn't feel anything.

Finally, on his way up, he felt little Billy's arms locked in a death grip on one of the posts of the dock, about 4 feet underwater. Prying the boy's fingers loose, they burst up together, through the surface to fill their lungs with life giving air. Finally, when the adrenaline had stopped surging and nerves had calmed down a bit, the Father asked his son, "What on earth were you doing down there hanging onto the post so far under the water?" Little Billy's answer was classic, laced with the wisdom only a toddler could give. He said, "I was just waiting for you dad. Just waiting for you."

Have you ever felt like you were going through the motions of life? And even though you couldn't quite put your finger on it, you continually felt as though there was something more to experience? Always feeling that somehow, a piece of the puzzle was missing in your life?

Yes, you have probably experienced many milestones. Such as buying a car and a house, getting married and raising a family. Maybe, you even have that little convertible you always wanted, parked in the garage. But, in your inner person, way down deep in your soul, you can't help but think, something is missing.

You're not alone, if you have ever thought or felt this way. I believe everyone experiences this phenomenon! I believe some are willing to admit this longing sensation, while far too many fight, ardently opposing it every step of the way. To search, find and experience what their soul consistently longs and hungers for!

The Bible says, God knew us before we were ever born and yet has witnessed and has been involved, in our entire lives!

> Psalms 139:16 TLB —*You saw me before I was born and scheduled each day of my life before I began to breathe. Every day was recorded in your book!*
>
> Jeremiah 1:5 NIV —*Before I formed you in the womb I knew you, before you were born I set you apart; I appointed you as a prophet to the nations.*

And while we were not all appointed to be prophets, preachers and teachers, God is not a respecter of persons, and according to the above scripture, every person has been known to God.

It's an amazing revelation and discovery! No matter where your relationship is with the Lord, no one can deny this truth about their existence! Even if you're not a Christian, before you entered into this world, God knew you! Each and every person, has already known, or has had the experience and some kind of remembrance of a relationship with God! It's no wonder why we feel like something is missing in our spiritual lives! Because it is!!

Whether or not we are appointed to be a prophet, we have already had a relationship and have been appointed, I believe, to have a relationship of reunification with our creator! The Bible clearly states we indeed have already been in the presence of God at conception!

Imagine you were taking a walk and discovered someone sitting with their back to you, turning around and realizing that someone was Jesus. What do you think His response would be if you were to ask Him what He was doing there? **I think Jesus would say to you, "I've been waiting for you child of God,** just waiting for you!"

What would you say to Jesus? What do you think the topic of conversation would be about? Would you have plenty in common through your relationship to talk with Jesus about?

Most people, who would find themselves in this situation, would probably be a little bit nervous, myself included! I mean come on, we're talking about Jesus, the Savior of the world, the One in charge of dispersing lavishly His Father's Goodness, sitting right before you, ready to listen and chat with you. You might be surprised!

And you might be surprised to discover you have a lot more in common with Jesus than you think. Even if you don't feel you are deserving to ask or receive anything, I imagine Jesus would still say you are!

> Luke 5:18-20 NKJV *Then behold, men brought on a bed a man who was paralyzed, whom they sought to bring in and lay before Him.* 19 *And when they could not find how they might bring him in, because of the crowd, they went up on the housetop and let him down with his bed through the tiling into the midst before Jesus.* 20 *When He saw their faith, He said to him, "Man, your sins are forgiven you."*

Jesus had exactly what the man needed. It doesn't say the man had faith, or he even asked for anything! Yet, **the commonality of the man's need and Jesus' willing ability to deliver, had an amazing conclusion!**

Jesus could have easily said to the man, "I've been waiting for you!" Jesus knew it, and I believe even though the paraplegic man may not have known, the man's friends knew it. That's why the man's friends went to so much trouble—to cut a hole in the roof of someone's house without permission—to arrange the man's healing encounter with Jesus!

Luke's account tells us Jesus recognized the man's friends, had faith, and Jesus acknowledged their faith! Even though Jesus acknowledged their faith, the man's friends weren't interested in taking any credit for what happened. They were only interested in the man's healing! Isn't that how we should all be?

When you love someone: A spouse, child, parent or friend and they're in need of a miracle, you really don't focus on the risks or potential backlash. **The only thing that matters is finding a way to get them the help and reward they so desperately need!**

When we are in search of a miracle, for whose glory are we seeking our miracle? Ourselves, or the ones we're praying for? Or are we ultimately seeking the glory of a higher power, the Light that guides us all?

When the paraplegic man's friends tore the roof apart, they weren't seeking recognition or fame. Whether they remained anonymous, or received gratitude didn't concern them; they were driven by selfless love. After the mountains of our need have been pushed aside and into the sea to disappear, what happens to the glory? **Who do we credit for a miracle? Who *should* we give the credit to?**

Jesus could have easily spoken any of the miracles He performed into existence, while He was here on earth and received all the glory! But He didn't! What Jesus chose to do instead was to glorify His Father! All the glory for every good thing on our behalf, or anyone else, belongs to God and no one else!

Lord knows, we in society have no problem blaming God for all kinds of things, when things go wrong. How is it, the world has such a hard time sharing the credit and the glory with God, when things go right?

Jesus understood human nature better than anyone! Jesus not only helped create all the complexities of human anatomy (by the way, science has yet to totally figure it all out), as well as the ability to decide and choose. Jesus also lived and experienced all of life's complexities, exactly as they were created!

What Jesus said in Matthew 19:26, Mark 10:27 and Luke 18:27, was the key! Jesus looked at them and gave them some great advice! Jesus said: "with man, this is impossible, but not with God; all things are possible with God."

The very same God who:
- parted the Red Sea,
- caused the walls of Jericho to fall, with a trumpet and a shout,
- healed the sick, by the thousands,
- raised the dead on many occasions,
- was tempted, by every known temptation, and was not overcome, but was victorious over them,
- performs miracles still today, on a regular basis, if you can and will believe!

While each and every one of those scenarios and stories from the Bible are almost beyond believability, they all happened! *They all happened!* And the reason they all happened, was because they all hinged on the moment in the relationship when it "got real!" In that one moment of faith, with the God of all things possible, is what turned their tide of need! **In that moment, they realized not that God could help them, but that God was willing and wanted to help them!**

If you're constantly worried about what's happening, or not happening in your life, because you think it's something that you can control yourself, I've got news for you, and it's not good! As long as you make your relationship with Jesus about what you are capable of on your own, you never will experience all that God has for you!

You see, no one has a hard time praising God, as long as they like what's happening to them! That's not giving total Glory to God! The Bible says *God works all things together for those who love Him, and are called to His purpose!*

Remember the Bible says God shares His glory with no one! Giving glory to God is found when you're able to praise and thank Him, even in the midst of the storm, when your faith is all there is to hang onto. That's being called to His purpose! It's an all in position of faith! When you praise and thank God, no matter what happens, or what the outcome is!

That's the way God wants you, who belong to Christ Jesus, to live. Yes, it's hard during times of testing, extremely hard! And it's in those extremely hard times, when we examine what happened, in retrospect.

We discover that we were far too dependent on our own self effort, rather than depending on our calling and God's amazing goodness, always available to us in unlimited portions!

I want you to listen, because this is important! The devil knows, better than anyone else, that what I'm about to tell you is true! The lying, worthless, conniving deceiver knows. When you're in relationship with Jesus, you're in the safety zone, under His umbrella of protection. As long as you're relying on His willingness, ability and power to help you, instead of your own, you're safe!! And there's absolutely nothing Satan can do about it!

It's an amazing feeling, knowing you're safe, no matter what comes your way. Because of the relationship you have with Jesus, you don't have to take a seat in the back of the bus, or settle for a life of mediocrity! You're in charge of your destiny. You won't have to listen to the devil's condemnation message at all! Jesus will fight your battles and willingly take care of all your needs, regardless of what they are!

Please realize once and for all, ***JESUS IS ALL YOU WILL EVER NEED***—
- no matter what you are facing today,
- no matter what's going on in the world around you,
- no matter what anybody says, friends or foes,
- no matter what the media reports,
- no matter what someone has done to you, stole from you, or said about you,
- no matter what economic advisors are predicting,
- no matter what your doctor is saying,
- no matter what your family is saying, or anyone else.

You should always be thanking and praising God, **and realize** the victory is already in your mouth! Far too many people don't know or act like it, but Jesus has already made them/us victorious over every situation! Will it always be an easy thing to do? Praising and thanking God in all circumstances? No, it will not always be an easy thing to do! In fact, most times, it may be the hardest thing to do in each and every part of life's circumstances that we face!

But I can tell you, from experience, praising with a heart of thanksgiving, is not as hard as the devil makes it out to be either! But, but, BUT will always be, every time, hands down, the most beneficial, and productive act of obedience we can do in every situation we face!

> Jeremiah 17:7-8 NKJV — *Blessed is the man who trusts in the LORD, And whose hope is the LORD. For he shall be like a tree planted by the waters, Which spreads out its roots by the river, And will not fear when heat comes; But its leaf will be green, And will not be anxious in the year of drought, Nor will cease from yielding fruit.*

Now sing:

> I shall not be, I shall not be moved.
> I shall not be, I shall not be moved.
> Just like a tree that's planted by the waters,
> I shall not be moved!

Yes that's an old song… but if you don't know that one, choose a song you do know about the goodness of God, and **start singing and believing God is going to do what you're asking!**

You see, no matter what song you sing, you should believe what the words declare, like a spiritual anthem of nothing is impossible! Or why would you even sing them in the first place? We must start believing like we're not responsible for the results we are asking for, but, **BUT believe** like God is both willing and responsible—with unlimited resources, of **guaranteed payment**!

Far too many Christians have been singing about the answers they're in need of for years and years! And at some point, we have to ask ourselves, do we really believe what we have heard and sang about for years and years? **Is the Power of God real in our lives, or simply words on a piece of paper, put to a nice little melody?**

Will you always feel like singing a praise song to God, when you get the news and the challenge you are sitting alone and facing? They can feel like a mountain parked on your front door step. I'm going to go out on a limb here and suggest, you're probably not going to feel like singing about the goodness of God at that moment!

Sing anyways! For Pete's sake, what do you have to lose? ***Sing anyways! Sing, sing, sing, through your sorrow. Sing through your brokenness, Sing through your struggle!* Sing about the goodness of God at the top of your lungs!** Sing before, during and after, even when you're right smack dab in the middle of your dilemma!

Sing the praises of God louder than you ever have before! ***Sing so obnoxiously loud,*** the devil is going to need earplugs to block your good singing and ***your testimony*** of faith that you're proclaiming and speaking over your situation!

Sing out in confidence, knowing Philippians 1:6 was written just for you, with one reason in mind. So you could be an ***overcomer!*** Say, *"I'm an **overcomer!**"* Repeat it with me... out loud as you are reading, *I'm an Overcomer! I'm an Overcomer!* ***I'm... An...OVERCOMER!*** *Not because of who I am, but because of who I Believe Jesus is, and what Jesus will accomplish through me and in me!*

> Phil. 1:6 HCSB — *I am sure of this, that He who started a good work in you will carry it on to completion until the day of Christ Jesus.*

I don't know about you, but there is great comfort to be found in that He who started a good work, will finish what He started! Philippians 1:6 is a word that you can stand on! A promise, a declaration, and a word, straight from the heart of heaven, that you can and should be depending on!

* When the going gets tough.
* When trouble is knocking relentlessly on your door.
* When everyone around you says you're facing an impossible situation.
* When you've done all you know to do and don't know what to do, kind of word!
* When you need to find strength to encourage yourself at times no one else can.

I believe this word right here, given to me by God for you today, is a word that's been waiting for you! You might say, I've heard this all before. Really? **Please tell me why we always find it hard to do, what we know we should be doing?**

This is a predestined moment in time! **Grab this word and this moment** and *Run Towards the Light!* If you will **grab a hold of this declaration and hang on** with the *more-than-enough measure of faith* you have, Jesus will change your life. You're now thinking of what is possible in your relationship with Him! **Dare to believe, dare to declare and dare to grab onto, and dare to never let go** of this life changing word!

We don't fight for victory today, praise God! We fight from Jesus' supernatural, super powerful, more than enough, death defying, already achieved and glorious victory over the cross, death, hell and the grave!

This amazing knowledge, the accuser never wants you, or anyone to realize. You have always had access to what Jesus accomplished for you! Access to this very same power!! Praise God!! Your relationship with Jesus has, is and will always give you access to the Power and Glory of God! If that **doesn't make you want to shout**, then nothing ever will.

So many Christians never fully realize how they can put the Word of God to work in their lives! We—but more importantly *I say— I SAY—* (make this personal). I say "I can reign over every situation, with the Lord's help, I can overcome every obstacle in MY life, instead of being held prisoner by them!"

You can, you can!

You can have access to this promise! Grab it once and for all! You can claim God's promise! You can have the promise you are entitle to because of your relationship with Jesus!

Life and death are in the power of the tongue! *Your tongue is a rudder.* **Let your tongue start guiding you—guiding you to what God has promised is possible, instead of constantly running you aground!**

With God's help, you are in charge, by the authority Jesus delivered—the authority He has given to you—over your circumstances! Start using what Jesus died to give to you! Don't let what Jesus has done, and is still doing for you, be in vain!

Start speaking God's word to your situations and to the situations of the ones around you. Your family, your friends, even complete strangers, those who God puts in your everyday travels. They need someone to speak this life changing word into their situation!

Quit telling the accuser everything that's wrong in your life. Instead, start proclaiming everything that's right! **Now you say it, Repeat at least three times!**

> *"I quit telling the accuser everything that's wrong with my life and I will proclaim everything that's right instead!"*

If Jesus is the Lord of your life, then you must believe Jesus has the greatest authority in your life. Jesus will help you continually overcome everything that will ever try to come against you! If you don't know Jesus today, in the way that we've been talking about Him so far, you can! **You can! You can! Jesus wants to know you, and have this kind of relationship with you!**

If your relationship is not where it should be today, it can be. Just pray and ask this—

> **Jesus, bring me into alignment, total alignment with the truth I've learned today!** I don't just want you to be the Lord of my heart, I want you to be the Lord over my life and over everything in my life! Help me break every Stronghold and Agreement I've ever had, with anything contrary to your Word, and be Lord over all I have!

Great! Now that we have that out of the way, we can move on! I will let you know, in the future, there will be upcoming tests, by the accuser's design! Tests that will challenge everything you've learned. Tests that will help grow your faith! I'm sure you'll do fine, with the Holy Spirit's ability, helping you recall what you need exactly at the right time!

In the meantime, let's uncover some other amazing discoveries—one's the accuser has hidden for far too long from God's people—discoveries you might not believe. But they're not over your head, they are already under your feet!

CHAPTER 3

IT'S NOT OVER YOUR HEAD—IT'S UNDER YOUR FEET.

Throughout the years, there have been many debatable dilemmas. Many like to think their viewpoint is as easy to see as the handwriting on the wall. So many different opinions to choose from. What seems right to one person seems noticeably wrong to another.

Are you an introvert or an extrovert? Are you an insider or an outsider? Pragmatist or visionary? Overachiever or underachiever? Are you on one side of the fence or the other side of the fence? Are you left-handed or right handed? Optimist or pessimist? Hot or cold?

The list of questions is long, as to what seems right and wrong in the world we live in! But the biggest controversy of all time, believe it or not, are you ready for this? It's…the debate, (drum roll please) it's the age old debate over toilet paper! Are you laughing? Not laughing? Well! Are you an over or an under the roll person in your household? There have been many debates and many disagreements over this simple necessity! And while we may laugh at this silly dilemma, the over and under part in the subconscious thinking, translates to an endless supply of things in life that are constantly fighting for our limited attention span.

But more importantly, in our everyday life, this simple act of choice of will that God has given to all of us, translates into our spiritual life. How you may ask? Through our decision to use or not use our faith, to our God given advantage, on an everyday basis!

There is an old saying, "don't sweat the small stuff in life, and it's all small." **Sometimes, we like to assign measured degrees of faith.** We think our individual needs may require us to have Jesus meet our needs! **Luke records Jesus' response, when the disciples inquired as to needing more or less faith:**

> Luke 17:6 MSG — *But the Master said, "You don't need more faith. There is no 'more' or 'less' in faith. If you have a bare kernel of faith, say the size of a poppy seed, you could say to this sycamore tree, 'Go jump in the lake,' and it would do it.*

I believe Jesus was the one who originally coined the above phrase, about sweating the small stuff! Because truly, anything you may be facing, while seemingly large to you, are most decidedly small to Jesus' amazing ability and equally amazing plan that He has for your life!

> Ephesians 1:15-23 NKJV —*Therefore I also, after I heard of your faith in the Lord Jesus and your love for all the saints,* 16 *do not cease to give thanks for you, making mention of you in my prayers:* 17 *that the God of our Lord Jesus Christ,* **the Father of glory, may give to you the spirit of wisdom and revelation in the knowledge of Him,** 18 **the eyes of your understanding being enlightened; that you may know what is the hope of His calling, what are the riches of the glory of His inheritance in the saints,** 19 **and what is the exceeding greatness of His power toward us who believe, according to the working of His mighty power** 20 **which He worked in Christ when He raised Him from the dead and seated Him at His right hand in the heavenly places,** 21 *far above all principality and power and might and dominion, and every name that is named, not only in this age but also in that which is to come.* 22 *And He put all things under His feet, and gave Him to be head over all things to the church,* 23 *which is His body, the fullness of Him who fills all in all.*

While our needs may seem to always be over our heads, they have never been over Jesus' head and His ability! The apostle Paul wanted us to come to the continual realization found in the words of Revelation, which he gave to the church at Ephesus!

It's not by our might, ability or effort, our needs are able to be met. **It is by the mighty power of the Great God Almighty, through His Son Jesus Christ, and through the relationship we have with Jesus, and the Amazing Holy Spirit of God, which lives in us!**

Have you ever watched a prerecorded football game where you knew the outcome of the game before you watched it? If your team was down by several points in the second quarter, or the third quarter, or even going into the fourth quarter, did it bother you? I'm going to venture to say this would not have bothered you. Because you would've known the outcome of the game and what was going to happen! Even though you didn't know how the turnabout would come to happen, you knew certain plays, events, and calls were going to turn the game around in your favor. No matter how things may have looked at any given moment. Ultimately, the knowledge you held, allowed you to remain calm and wait for what you had already been told was going to happen.

That's what Paul is saying here. Paul is wanting to let us know and realize exactly what you've been given. How amazingly well God has equipped you, to deal with anything the accuser or life may throw at you.

Paul, but more importantly, his writing, is what the inspired word of God wants you to know and understand. No matter what stage of need you are facing! You don't have to worry about your needs being too much for Jesus to handle, **because Jesus has been given charge over all things, and all things are under His feet!**

* Jesus is your greatest advocate!
* Jesus is your portion!
* Jesus is your protector!
* Jesus is your provider!
* Jesus is your financier!
* Jesus is your Healer!
* Jesus will be your everything in every situation you expect Him to be!

In a nutshell, we realize through our relationship with Jesus, that our needs, however great or small, are not over Jesus' head! And ultimately, if they're not over Jesus' head, they're not over our head either! This line of thinking, which God gave to Paul, lets us know, and makes us continually aware of Jesus' ability and desire to help us!

Our relationship with Jesus is so multifaceted, because our relationship covers every aspect of our lives! Everything from our spiritual needs, to physical and emotional needs, right down to our immense need to love and be loved!

God cared so much for the world! **God, so loved the world and everything He created! So much so, that He sent His only son Jesus, to establish a way of relationship** and a way to not only meet the world's physical needs, but to supernaturally meet and exceed them all. And to be the only victory over death that the world would ever have!

Recognize any of these words? "We hold these truths to be self-evident, that all men are created equal, that they are endowed by their Creator with certain unalienable Rights, that among these are Life, Liberty and the pursuit of Happiness."

Yes, that's right. That is the Declaration of Independence. And our founding fathers absolutely knew the enormity of what they had been given by God Himself, when this country became a country. So, they declared and made a record of it. They wrote it down, so the knowledge at the time of the event would never be forgotten!

Under the divine inspiration of the Holy Spirit, Ben, Thomas, Alexander, Samuel...wrote it down! We still have the document to protect and preserve what they declared for our freedom, so long ago! **They collectively realized the enormity of what God gave them, preserved the moment for generations, and declared it forever!**

Have you made your spiritual declaration? Have you really gotten a hold of, and do you really realize, what you have been given by the creator of the universe? Everything the Bible declares, and by His Promises, that you have been given?

David, whose words we are about to read, at some point in time, realized and had a life changing epiphany! He realized what he, by his relationship with God, had been given to him! And exactly what God's promise gives to all of us when we make the same realization!

> Psalms 139 NKJV — *O Lord, You have searched me and known me.* 2 **You know my sitting down** *and my rising up;* **You understand my thoughts afar off.** 3 *You comprehend my path and my lying down, And are acquainted with all my ways.*
> 4 *For there is not a word on my tongue, But behold, O Lord, You know it altogether.* 5 *You have hedged me behind and before, And laid Your hand upon me.* 6 *Such knowledge is too wonderful for me; It is high, I cannot attain it.* 7 **Where can I go from Your Spirit? Or where can I flee from Your presence?** 8 *If I ascend into heaven, You are there; If I make my bed in hell, behold, You are there.* 9 *If I take the wings of the morning, And dwell in the uttermost parts of the sea,* 10 **Even there Your hand shall lead me, And Your right hand shall hold me.** 13 *For You formed my inward parts; You covered me in my mother's womb.* 16 **Your eyes saw my substance, being yet unformed. And in Your book they all were written, The days fashioned for me, When as yet there were none of them.** 17 *How precious also are Your thoughts to me, O God! How great is the sum of them!*

If you have never understood how much God is, and wants to be, involved in your life, you should now! If not read this amazing Psalm again. Every child of God needs to insert their name and realize David's discovery can, and should, be your realization as well.

This is David's declaration of faith and acknowledgment of God's greatness. And it displays well how God amazingly made and equipped David to live life! **David knew who he was and what he had been given, because of his willingness to walk by faith and in relationship with God! You can too, friend. God wants the very same intimacy of relationship with you! He longs for you to walk with Him just as David did!**

How do we know he knew this? Because David declared by acknowledging and writing it down! Not just for us to see, but for everyone, forever to see his declaration of faith and relationship with

God! Imagine the effect David's revelation has had on the church? More importantly, how has David's revelation now shaped your thinking and life?

Imagine also, never one time did David experience Jesus' Grace, or Salvation! David lived his entire life under the covenant of the law! How much more should we believe and declare, since we have been given the gift of salvation by Jesus, His deliverance of grace and way of relationship through His own relationship, with His Father God!

Shouldn't we realize and learn from David's example of declaration, what is available and possible through our relationship with Jesus, when we put our faith and trust in Him? The answer is a resounding, "**Yes, my friends!**"

> Isaiah 52:7 MSG — *How beautiful on the mountains are the feet of the messenger bringing good news, Breaking the news that all's well, proclaiming good times, announcing salvation, telling Zion, "Your God reigns!"*

Listen, you don't have to be a pastor or a preacher, to share the good news of the gospel! All you have to do is share your own Jesus story! Everybody who claims to be a Christian, has a story! **Start living your life unafraid, like your testimony is your declaration of Faith! Because it is!** If it's not, don't you think it should be?

What are the truths in your life you're making and declaring about your faith and relationship with Jesus? The Bible says what comes out of your mouth, comes into your life! In essence, your own words speak into existence your future!

Don't be afraid to speak life over your circumstances. Let your words align with the promises of God, and watch as transformation takes shape.

Do you believe what the Bible says about your inheritance and what your expectation should be from the relationship you have with Jesus? Yes, or no? What do I mean, yes or no? This is not a hard question to answer. Either you believe what the scriptures declare and the promises for your life, or you don't!

If your answer is yes, then take your God given authority and start living the AMAZING life Jesus has given to you! "Nothing you will ever face in life will ever be over your head, because everything is already under your feet!" Because they are under Jesus' feet!!!

What are some declarations of truth in your relationship with Jesus that you have been given? By the gospel message of grace, are you aware of the declarations of truth, you as a believer, are entitled to? **Have you ever written any of them down?** Really? Why not? I think you should! Because they will empower your position of faith!

God is faithful! Do you believe this part of the time? Or all the time? God is true, God is good. God is caring and loving. God is always attentive to all of your needs. God is always in control of every situation. Do you believe God has given Jesus absolute authority and the final say in every matter? Even the critical, mountain-sized needs you're unable to figure out concerning your future?

Do you know exactly who you are to God? Do you believe you are His child? Do you believe no matter what happens, or what you have done or may ever do, you are and will always be loved by God?

Do you believe that even before you were in your mother's womb, you were chosen by God? That you were a beloved son or daughter of the most high God? Are you aware that you are in God's thoughts every moment of every day? Are you aware you are on Jesus' radar screen at all times and are Jesus' continual concern?

Our lives are not a bunch of individual stories being written and scattered throughout the universe! The story of us, the story of God, is the story of Jesus in the world!

Every one of us, *even you my friend*, are a part of Jesus' story! Our future, and the next chapter of our story, and the chapter after, if we will believe and declare, can be....will be wonderful! An amazing, unbelievable story with an amazing, over the top, and unbelievable ending! It's just waiting to be told and fully realized! A story, yes your story my friend, with an amazing conclusion no eye has ever seen, and no ear has ever heard!

Can you say these words with confidence, realizing, truthfully, that this is all you will ever need to know? **You, my dear reader, have been given the ability to have the exact same relationship, or one even better than the author of these words, had with the Creator of all. The One True Living God!**

> Psalms 23:1, 6 NKJV —*The Lord is my shepherd; I shall not want…. Surely goodness and mercy shall follow me all the days of my life; And I will dwell in the house of the Lord Forever.*

It's no wonder, Psalms 23 is a favorite Psalm of so many people! Not only those who are in the church, but in general! I believe the reason being, Psalms 23 is a Psalm of dependency! Not dependency on self, **but by one's total realization and dependency on God's ability and God's ability alone!**

David applied his declaration of Faith behind the words he penned in Psalms 23, to every need great and small, over his entire life! Yes, David had great victories, David also had moments of setback! Just like you and I do in our walk and relationship with Jesus in our own lives! Yet, God said, David was a man after his own heart!

The Bible says that God is not a respecter of persons. So apply your declarations of faith to your relationship with God; it's the same God David served!

God will write in His book of remembrances the same thing He wrote about David, and, I believe, about so many others throughout the history of the world! Is your name written in God's book of remembrances that way? If not, your name can be! **If you've never aligned your way of thinking with God's way of thinking, why not start today?** Know and realize, there's nothing above your pay grade of qualification, when your relationship with Jesus takes center stage in your life!

The more you align yourself and bring your thinking into unity with God's way of thinking, the more you realize, as you "Run Towards the Light", that there is nothing God is not willing to do for one of His children!

CHAPTER 4

THE POWERFUL VOICE OF UNITY

When I think about the word unity, the song Russ Taff wrote so many years ago, rings continually in the back of my mind! Because we, the church, talk about being unified and becoming the powerful army God has called us to be. But we continually sit idly by, when we truthfully know the word unity is and has always been, in its meaning, an action word! Unifying two or more personalities takes an unbelievable amount of work! And I want to be part of that movement, not just in word, but in deed. I believe the word unity should be a verb. Because it is an interactive word and should be, in my opinion, an action word!

Read the lyrics that Russ Taff wrote, and see if I can't persuade you to agree with what is possible when we take some initiative in our interactions to come together in one giant voice of unity!

> You're my brother, you're my sister,
> So take me by the hand,
> Together we will work until He comes.
> There's no foe that can defeat us,
> When we're walking side by side.
> As long as there is love, we will stand.

And what we do together for the kingdom, is going to be the only thing that will stand for eternity! What will unite us together and cause all believers to work side by side, with one common goal? Only one thing comes to mind. **Only the love of God could ever accomplish something of that magnitude!** Only if we love God and each other, as Jesus spoke were the two greatest commandments above all others, will we ever advance and achieve what we have been called to do!

> Ephesians 4:1-5 NKJV — *I, therefore, the prisoner of the Lord, beseech you to walk worthy of the calling with which you were called, 2 with all lowliness and gentleness, with longsuffering, bearing with one another in love, 3 endeavoring to keep the unity of the Spirit in the bond of peace. 4 There is one body and one Spirit, just as you were called in one hope of your calling; 5 one Lord, one faith, one baptism; 6 one God and Father of all, who is above all, and through all, and in you all.*

Sometimes, I wonder, how many of God's children are truly aware of the strength such unity can bring? The Bible, from the beginning, was assimilated to help all of us find the answers to the questions life presents! Paul said, I beseech [to urgently, and fervently plead a case] you, to walk worthy of the calling with which you were called! This is not a general letter Paul was writing to just anyone. **Paul, was and is, speaking directly to those who call themselves Christians. This is for you and me.** This word is not meant to be passed on to someone else! This is meant for each one of us to take deeply into our hearts, to ponder, to meditate upon, and to live out through our testimonies, in our daily lives!

I remember hearing the story of a 5-year-old little boy named Jimmy, who was playing with his 2-year-old brother Johnny, one day. When suddenly the 2-year old reached up and yanked his older brother's hair. Jimmy screamed in pain, and his mother came rushing in. He cried and said that his younger brother Johnny had pulled his hair.

His mom said, "Well, he's only 2 years old and he doesn't know what it's like to have his hair pulled." The mom left and seconds later she heard a scream from the bedroom, but this time it was the 2-year old screaming in pain. She rushed in and asked what had happened to Johnny? To which the 5-year old explained, "You said he didn't know what it felt like, well, now he does."

How many of you realize you didn't choose God? How many of you are aware that God chose you? If you didn't before, you do now!

> 1 Peter 2:9-10 MSG —*But you are the ones, [insert your name here], chosen by God, chosen for the high calling of priestly*

work, chosen to be a holy people, God's instruments to do his work and speak out for him, to tell others of the night-and-day difference he made for you, [insert your name again], from nothing to something, from rejected to accepted. The Holy Spirit gently called you into salvation and to a life long walk of relationship with the One who created you. If you never realized you were called before by God Himself, again I say, now you do!

I want you to realize how amazingly special you are to God and how much God loves you today! In fact, if that's all you came to know from reading this book, that realization alone will liberate you and set you free to pursue your calling like never before!

In the same breath, I want you to know we haven't been called to walk this journey alone, but for a glorious partnership with the divine. We have all been called to work together with Jesus, for the Glory of God!

When we all come together in unity and share the responsibility of what God has called us to do, when we look to God to deliver all the results, without expectation of receiving credit, the results will be beyond what we could have ever hoped or imagined! This perspective of responsibility is liberating! Because when you only look to God as your source, **you realize you're not the one responsible for results, God is, God always has been, God always will be!**

This freedom allows you to set your bar of faith higher each and every time you pray! Thus, releasing greater and larger faith than you ever could imagine is possible! This freedom will allow you to do what Jesus said was possible, "Greater things shall you do!" Jesus' words echoed, as He ascended to heaven.

Results have never been up to us! We will never be in charge of the timing and or delivery of results! But results are exactly what we're always looking for! The only lasting and countable results we should be looking for, is to take as many souls to heaven with us as possible! One day we will receive our reward, when we lay our accomplishments—our crowns, our trophies—at Jesus' feet. **I don't know about you, but on that day, I would like to have a great assortment of crowns and trophies to give to Jesus!**

Don't play down your ability or what God expects from you to deliver! God is **raising up an army of conquerors** and that's exactly how you should see yourself—the same way God does! How you see yourself matters! *God sees you as an overcomer and that's how God wants you to see yourself!*

We don't live in a microwave society; we live in a nanosecond world! And every opportunity, every prayer, every poppy seed size of Faith, everything we do matters! **We have an incredible opportunity before us as a body of believers. I want to talk a little further about the power of unity and the *huge* opportunity to win souls, that is standing wide open before us.**

We have asked, we have believed, we have prayed. We have questioned both God and each other about the harvest of souls we would like to see come into the family of God—into the church. Not just joining a mega church, but becoming part of the local church, **where the rubber meets the road of needs in the lives of people!** Nothing against the mega churches, mind you, but Jesus said to go to the highways and the byways and gather as many as possible for the marriage supper of the Lamb! Some people suggest: "Well Charlie, all you're interested in is numbers." Yes, I am interested in numbers, but not the kind of numbers they're referring to.

I am interested in the numbers Jesus said to go after! The incalculable number of people the Devil's got a hold of, and are on a highway to hell! The people that don't stand a chance and aren't going to make it to heaven. We, who know, need to put action behind our words, and do whatever necessary to win them from the devil's stranglehold, and bring them to the gift of salvation and forgiveness in Christ Jesus!

The Apostle Paul strongly suggests to compel the ones who need Jesus, to go and reach them with the Message of the cross and forgiveness! The gift of Salvation Jesus sacrificed His life to give them, by whatever means necessary.

What does *compel* mean to you?

The word, *"com-pel"* is a verb. That means it is an action word. To force or oblige someone to do something.

To: force, coerce into, pressure, impel, drive, plead with, press, push, urge, prevail on, oblige, require, put under an obligation, leave someone no option but to, make, twist someone's arm, etc.

All of these are descriptions that Google gave me, similar to the word *compel*. And why would we not do a lot of them? Maybe intimidation or fear, I'm guessing? Maybe we're afraid someone might call us a Jesus fanatic, God forbid. I don't know about you, but I would consider being called a fan of Jesus a compliment. For too many of us, the fact is, we're guilty of not doing any of them. Why is that? Why do we have such a hard time presenting the gospel?

Friend, if you can't tell everything Jesus has done for you, can't you at least share something Jesus has done for you? Your story is much more compelling than you think it is! **The irony is, your story is very similar to everyone else's story, who has been liberated from a lifetime of sin! And you might just find this to be true, if you would be willing to tell and share your story. The story within the story of Jesus and how He found you and saved you. How Jesus Rescued you from a spiritual destination of the pit of hell and torment!** I mean, shouldn't our personal story be one we can tell passionately? To share what Jesus has done for us? And shouldn't we want to tell it as often as we can? Shouldn't that be the most refreshing and important piece of news we share everyday?

We, as believers, have asked, believed, and prayed for the harvest of souls we want to see come into our local churches. Up until this point, for the most part, we have done all those things individually as a singular voice, rather than a unified body of storytellers. Unified collectively in faith, **each of us willing to share our own life changing stories,** expectantly believing for the harvest of souls God has promised from our obedience of doing so.

> Matthew 9:35-37 NKJV — 35 *Then Jesus went about all the cities and villages, teaching in their synagogues, preaching the gospel of the kingdom, and healing every sickness and every disease among the people.* 36 *But when He saw the multitudes, He was moved with compassion for them, because they were weary and scattered, like sheep having*

no shepherd. 37 But when He saw the multitudes, He was moved with compassion for them.

Put on your spiritual glasses, go out, and look in the places you frequent. You cannot help but see, even 2000 years later, the exact same thing Jesus saw. There are still hurting people everywhere. There are still confused people. There are still people hungry for answers! I mean, if you have never people-watched before, I suggest you take a day and observe what's going on around you, Take a moment to focus on the world around you, instead of your own set of issues.

Open your spiritual eyes, and what you will find are people, desperately looking for love, hope, acceptance and satisfaction from whatever source they can find. All the while, not knowing that the answers they're searching for, are and can only be found in Jesus. ***You are the one God wants to send to show them the way!***

Jesus gave the charge…"Then He said to His disciples, The harvest truly is plentiful, but the laborers are few. Therefore pray the Lord of the harvest to send out laborers into His harvest."

So many churches, and entire denominations, have forgotten **we are all on the same team, and we all serve the same God. Too many in the church have forgotten it is their relationship, and that God is the only one who has a scoreboard, that matters!** So much influence of religious tradition, so many personal different agendas without the focus of unity, to put numbers on God's scoreboard alone, instead of their own.

One person of unity, Jesus, and one **unified** Church, Jesus' body of believers, will never be able to complete the task Jesus has challenged us all to do, *if* we don't become unified in one resounding voice of relationship and call, to start fighting in unity together against the kingdom of darkness!

Unity defined:
1. The state or quality of being one; singleness
2. The state or quality of being in accord; harmony
3. The combination or arrangement of parts into a whole; unification
4. Singleness or constancy of purpose or action; continuity: "In an army you need unity of purpose"

In God's army, we need the same thing. There is strength in unity.

> Ecclesiastes 4:12 NKJV — *Though one may be overpowered by another, two can withstand him. And a threefold cord is not quickly broken.*

Just how much strength, the Bible says. God has given us enough strength to withstand the challenges ahead, where nothing will be impossible, as long as we are in His will. **Everything ever achieved and considered great throughout all of history, has had the unity of each participant's measure of God-given faith, involved as the main ingredient and common denominator.** Read it again!

> Acts 2:1-4 NKJV — *When the Day of Pentecost had fully come, they were all with one accord in one place. 2 And suddenly there came a sound from heaven, as of a rushing mighty wind, and it filled the whole house where they were sitting. 3 Then there appeared to them divided tongues, as of fire, and one sat upon each of them. 4 And they were all filled with the Holy Spirit and began to speak with other tongues, as the Spirit gave them utterance.*

Notice how all of them were in one accord, and they had been together in prayer and unity, for quite some time! Roughly 10 days, 240 hours and 14,400 minutes. ALL unified with the same purpose in mind! No separatism, or soloing efforts! **They were all hanging on to the promise Jesus left them with! They were all striving, seeking and praying together! One goal, with the same purpose in mind, all wanting the same thing!** If we could only cultivate such unity in our churches and in our own lives, imagine the miracles and wonders we could achieve. If we could only have the same spirit of unity, the disciples had!

Now, before we go on with this line of thinking, I want to refute all those who say, "that was a 'then moment' and this is a 'now moment', in church history!"

I know this is probably going to upset the apple cart of theological opinions! By that meaning, the Holy Ghost infilling and speaking in tongues experience doesn't happen anymore, or that's not what the church is about anymore.

First of all I would like to ask, by whose authority has such a statement been validated, to even be considered relevant? I would like to challenge this assumption, because the Spirit of God transcends time, pouring into all those who are willing to receive. Last time I checked, there has not been a recall of the promise found in Acts chapter 2, or any other chapters of the Bible!

Maybe your Bible says God's words, commands and actions stopped after a little while and God's plans and commands have stopped fulfilling what God asked of them… but I don't think it does! **My Bible, your Bible and every Bible says, God's words never return void until they have completed their assignment and what God has sent them and instructed them to do!** God's instructive words are still actively pursuing and working diligently, to achieve their assignment! God's plans have never stopped what they were instructed and expected to do and accomplish!

I want you to think about something. Are Jesus' actions that He took on the Cross, still paying for your sin? Still and continually affording you unlimited grace and the opportunity to go to heaven? If the answer is yes, then don't you think what the Lord gave us on the day of Pentecost and the power of the Holy Spirit that came with the gift is still working to complete God's will (His plans) through the Power of the Holy Spirit as well??

Those who were there on the day of Pentecost, were without a doubt, unified in their objective! And when the Holy Ghost fell that day, how many did He fall on? All, all of them! Praise God! The Holy Spirit fell on every single one of them! And the results sent shock waves around the world, still being felt today!

God will and wants to reward us in the very same way and that's exactly why the Holy Spirit came! Jesus said from the word and I quote, "greater things shall you do, because I go to my father and the comforter will be revealed!" **Jesus wants the Holy Spirit, sent by His Father, to pour out His Blessing on all of our efforts and to not hold anything back from us!** To enable and multiply our efforts, with His willingness to apply His Ability and Favor-Filled anointing of Blessing, to everything we attempt to do in His name!

The problem is, too many in the church have become NUMB TO THE WORD and the power of the word, grace! The church was once a vast domain of fertile soil, with an abundance of fruit produced! But through the relentless attack of the accuser, the church and far too many of the church body, THAT WERE once fertile soil, have become a barren land and a lifeless valley of dry bones!

And this is sad to say, but it's so true! Having a form of Godliness, but denying the power thereof! And by this, I mean... Taking the Bible, and the promises of God literally, and believing exactly what God has declared and promised throughout scripture, we can do and have been called to do!

The good news is, **it's not too late!** *It's not too late* **to change the course of what has become the status quo!** It's not too late for the church to experience an Ezekiel moment! I believe an Ezekiel moment in the waiting, is exactly where the church is! I believe we are on the cusp of, without a doubt, the greatest revival in the history of the church that we have ever seen! Are you, dear reader, ready to stand up and be counted in the ***Army of the Lord***?

> Ezekiel 37:7-10 MSG — *I prophesied just as I'd been commanded. As I prophesied, there was a sound and, oh, rustling! The bones moved and came together, bone to bone. I kept watching. Sinews formed, then muscles on the bones, then skin stretched over them. But they had no breath in them.* 9 *He said to me, "Prophesy to the breath. Prophesy, son of man. Tell the breath, 'God, the Master, says, Come from the four winds. Come, breath. Breathe on these slain bodies.* 10 *So I prophesied, just as he commanded me. The breath entered them and they came alive! They stood up on their feet, a huge army.*

[If you haven't read the story of Ezekiel, you should!]

If we are willing to join arms with each other, to tear down all religion's segregating and doctrinal walls, becoming united together as one army of believers, collectively taking up the cross of Jesus and doing what God asks us to do, **we can and should expect a harvest of souls which the Bible says we can't even begin to imagine.** Right now, imagine the greatest harvest possible! I want you to know, your expectations fall short and fail in comparison to what God wants to do!

This word of expectation is for such a time as this.

This word of expectation is not a word that somebody else, or so and so ought to hear. This is not a time to be thinking about what's for lunch, or the pain in your back, or how uncomfortable the chair is feeling right now that you're sitting on, or about what's going to happen tomorrow. For tomorrow will take care of itself.

This word is a wake-up call to let us know that if we don't do something today, lost souls will perish forever spending eternity in hell, by tomorrow!

Many years ago, when I was 19 years old, I had a dream. I was standing in a line going to heaven. Next to me, there was another line, going to hell.

And in the line going to hell, I recognized far too many people I could've shared Jesus with, but for one reason or another, chose not to. It was a sickening feeling to know their blood would be on my hands, if I didn't change my willingness to witness to them! Friend, I bring this up because I think we can all relate! If not today, when will we ever attempt to do what God has called us to? None of us are promised tomorrow, neither are our family, friends, or neighbors!

> Matthew 5:14-16 MSG — *Here's another way to put it: You're here to be light, bringing out the God-colors in the world. God is not a secret to be kept. We're going public with this, as public as a city on a hill. If I make you light-bearers, you don't think I'm going to hide you under a bucket, do you? I'm putting you on a light stand. Now that I've put you there on a hilltop, on a light stand— shine!*

Keep an open house; be generous with your lives. By opening up to others, you'll prompt people to open up with God, this generous Father in heaven.

This is a word for those who are reading right now. **This is a word for you, friend. For you!** Not someone else. You are not reading this book by accident! This is a divine appointment in the making! If you're ever going to grow, and grow the way I believe God wants us all to grow, and impact our communities!

We need to take the gospel message of light, that we have been given, and *get busy shining the light of Jesus, like we never have before!* The status quo, or the mentality of mediocrity, should be a description of words and a frame of mind, never accepted or settled for in our life, our relationship with Jesus, or in the church.

We like to read and to hear about all the great outpourings of the Holy Spirit. Especially what happened at the Azusa Street Revival. The common thread of all of them, just like on the day of Pentecost, was, still and will always be **unity of our faith**. All of the participants were sick and tired of the way things were! That feeling, and their hunger, caused them to come together in unity and by the act of continually seeking the Promise of the Holy Spirit, Jesus delivered and Historical accounts read, they all prayed and fasted for as long as it took. Then the windows of Heaven opened and the power of God fell—**power so strong that the effects are still reverberating around the world today.**

Illustrated in Bartleman's first account words, 'What really happened at Azusa Street' he states

> *Suddenly the Spirit would fall upon the congregation. God himself would give the altar call. Men would fall all over the house, like the slain in battle, or rush for the altar en masse to seek God. The scene often resembled a forest of fallen trees.... Some claim to have seen the [Shekhinah] glory by night over the building.*

Azusa Street happened in April of 1906, over 119 years ago, and people are still talking about what happened today! Still seeking and wanting to experience that experience! Can you blame them? I don't know about you, but I don't just want the church to talk about the experience anymore! We're all guilty of talking about wanting to experience the unbridled power of God, until we're blue in the face!

It's time to quit talking about experiencing the power of God. It's time we start seeking out and praying together in unity, for the Power of the

Holy Spirit that God has already given to us—compelling each other and believing for the Power of the Holy Spirit to happen again. And again. And again—enabling and empowering us, to be the army, God is raising up in this moment of time.

God is not, nor has He ever been a respecter of persons. The problem is, we tend to think God is! Friend, I'm going to tell you, the people who were there on the day of Pentecost, and the people that were there at Azusa Street, were not of affluent means....they all just wanted more of God! The time has come to forget about all the materialism of life and realize the only thing that matters and will hold water on the day of judgment, is what you accomplish for the Kingdom Of God!

We, *as a united body of believers, collectively* need to develop a stronger sense of hunger, to desire *as fully as we can*, what we are talking about here! Unity means to have the same goal, expecting the same results! **Wouldn't it be amazing if we could all come together as one gigantic force for the kingdom of God, with the one and only goal of bringing lost souls to Jesus!**

I read a story about two men who were riding a bicycle built for two, when they came to a big steep hill. It took a great deal of struggle for the men to complete what proved to be a very stiff climb. When they got to the top the man in front turned to the other and said, "Boy, that sure was a hard climb." Then the fellow in back replied, "Yes, and if I hadn't kept the brakes on all the way we would certainly have rolled down backwards."

Friend, it's time to fasten our spiritual seatbelt, take our foot off the brake, and start saying yes to the FAVOR of acceleration that God is calling us all to do. We must grab hold of the fact, what God has done down through the ages for the faith of others, He will do not just for some of us, but we must, **must, *must*** believe, for all of us. He will do EVEN GREATER THINGS, if we humble ourselves, pray and call on His name, unified together, hold on and not let go until the power of revival falls!

> Ephesians 1:19-20 NKJV — *And what is the exceeding greatness of His power toward us who believe, according to the working of His mighty power which He worked in*

Christ when He raised Him from the dead and seated Him at His right hand in the heavenly places.

I recently came across this cleverly worded poem. I believe all of us can relate, in one way or another, to the words:

There was a clever young guy named Somebody Else.

There is nothing Somebody Else can't do.

He is busy from morning till late at night,

Substituting doing this and that for you.

When you are asked to volunteer,

What is your ready reply?

Get Somebody Else to do that job.

He'll do it much better than I.

So much to do in this weary old world—

So much to do, and workers so few.

And Somebody Else, all weary and worn,

Is still substituting for... **Y O U**.

If we come together in unity, the same resurrection power that raised Jesus from the grave, we can all experience and have work in our lives. And the best part is, **it's completely sustainable and shareable power.**

We all have an awesome opportunity ahead of us, as we willingly lock arms. Marching unified together, with the resurrection power God has already, not one day, but has already made available to us. Praise God!

I want you to realize there is nothing, I repeat nothing, you/we can't accomplish for the glory and the story of Jesus in God's Kingdom. **Are you willing? Are you willing to be a part of and to do something greater than yourself, that has never been achieved for the kingdom of God?**

Then, let your prayer be...

"Father God, I willingly give what I have to you. I want You to take what I have, multiply it together and unite my faith, with my fellow brothers and sisters in Christ. Lord, I ask you to give back, with an abundance of noticeable fruit, to each and everyone willing to unite, to be Your hands, Your feet and Your voice. In such quantity, I may freely give away what you gave to me, even more abundantly than I have received. Shine Your light upon me, so I may light the path for others, who desperately need to see Your light. I thank You for helping me, to be who you've called me to be, and to do what you have asked me to do."

What a beautiful prayer! If that was you, my friend, I would suggest buying a journal, if you don't already have one.

Here's why. I believe God is getting ready to use you in a totally new and amazing way that you've never seen or experienced, as you continue to write your story, in to **the story of Jesus!**

CHAPTER 5

SOME PLANT, SOME WATER—WHICH ONE ARE YOU?

Ephesians 2:4-7, NKJV — But God, who is rich in mercy, because of His great love with which He loved us... raised us up together, and made us sit together in the heavenly places in Christ Jesus, that in the ages to come He might show the exceeding riches of His grace in His kindness toward us in Christ Jesus.

But God who is rich in mercy? Who doesn't love or want a God, who is rich in mercy? A brief biblical definition of mercy is "the gift of God's undeserved kindness and compassion." The word mercy is such an extraordinary, yet complex concept! So much so, the word **mercy** takes several Hebrew and Greek words, to express the dimensions of its meaning! **Synonyms like compassion, loving-kindness, favor and steadfast love, often appear in Bible translations to illustrate the idea of mercy.**

Only God could love us, fully, completely and unconditionally, without the possibility of us ever loving Him in return! Only a love like God's love, could have enough meaning and power behind it, to raise us up and make us sit together in the heavenly places, with Christ Jesus!

Friend, you might be wondering why I'm going through the litany of all this! It's because I want you to know why God went to all the trouble, to do what He did! "So, that in the ages to come, He might show the exceeding riches of His grace in His kindness toward us in Christ Jesus!"

What I want you to realize is, God has already created and completed all of His preparations in advance! So, whatever we would face, whenever we would have need, God could pour out His love for us, through exceedingly great quantities of His grace towards us and on us, in the ages to come! Which is right now, friend! **God's mercies are new every morning and today is the time to receive what God has already prepared for you to walk into and inhabit through His goodness!** In every moment going forward, in every way you will need!

Wow! Think about the immensity of God's goodness and of **this amazing promise we have been given!** Yes, we rejoice in what God has done in the past! Yes, we also rejoice in what God is going to do going forward into the future! And we look to the future with great anticipation, because we know Jesus is coming back triumphantly, for His bride! But my question today is, why aren't we looking for and rejoicing about what God is doing today?

As in the time-frame of *right now, today*, this very moment! **Not for what He has done, or what He is going to do, but for what God is doing right now!** Take the time to look through your kingdom glasses, for what the Holy Spirit is creating for you, in real time!

How is that possible, you might ask? Have you ever tried? I know from personal experience, if you try to look for the things God is doing for you in your life in real time, you will see the hand of God moving. If you **will look** I'm sure you will discover what He did. How amazing it is, to see God's plans working in your life, in the moment of now!

We know the magnitude of what God can do, for those who believe and expectantly in faith, call upon his name! Because we have heard and studied the amazing, sometimes bigger than life true stories, from the Bible.

* We know God parted the Red Sea,
* We know God rained fire down from Heaven and consumed Elijah's sacrifice,
* We know when Jesus prayed and called upon his Father, Jesus easily fed, multiplied, thousands of hungry people, with just a little boy's small lunch

* We know, because we have so many miraculous events God allowed to be witnessed in real time, *in the moment of now.*

When Jesus fed the thousands, Jesus didn't feed them with enough to suppress their appetite. Jesus fed and filled them, to the full! We all know, God has performed countless, amazing miracles throughout history, and it's important we give Him praise and glory for what He has done. But at the same time we also have to look forward to what God wants to do in the right NOW moment of today.

Paul was talking about and looking towards the future, not the past. The Bible says, in the ages to come, God would do things, far superseding anything God has ever done before. **The ages to come Paul is talking about, is the time we are living in right now.** God is a God of way too much, not a God of barely getting by. Let me say it again, with greater clarity. **God is a God of way, way too much!**

We need to quit thinking our prayers will be answered with a *Groundhog Day* mentality and a 50/50 answer of maybe. We need to consistently use our faith and pray every day that our prayers will be answered, as though it is our childlike faith and expectation of receiving Christmas morning blessings, every time.

When Jesus fed the five thousand, which really was more like 12 to 15 thousand with women and children, did Jesus give them a snack? *No... "He fed them!"* I mentioned they were hungry, right? Have you truly ever been hungry? **I think we could all agree, hungry people tend to eat more.** Right? The meal Jesus fed them, was without a doubt, the best fish I'm sure, by far, they had ever tasted. So therefore, they would've easily eaten, I believe, two to three times as much food as it would have taken to feed them, under normal circumstances.

Jesus answered their need, by the appetite or expectation of their need! Guess what, friend? *Jesus is willing to meet and answer our needs the exact same way.*

In the story of Jesus turning water into wine, Jesus created the best wine they had ever tasted, which might suggest the goodness of what I'm trying to convey here. Again, this Word is a little lengthy, but so amazingly powerful to convey Jesus' willingness to deliver!

John 2:6-10 MSG — *Six stoneware water pots were there, used by the Jews for ritual washings. Each held twenty to thirty gallons. Jesus ordered the servants, "Fill the pots with water." And they filled them to the brim. "Now fill your pitchers and take them to the host," Jesus said, and they did. When the host tasted the water that had become wine (he didn't know what had just happened but the servants, of course, knew), he called out to the bridegroom, "Everybody I know begins with their finest wines and after the guests have had their fill brings in the cheap stuff. But you've saved the best till now!"*

I want to ask you a question. Whose expectation did Jesus honor and answer by doing what He did here? If you said Mary, his mother's expectation, you would be correct.

I believe Jesus is always willing to take our expectations and multiply them with his ability and favor mindedness, to deliver more than what our expectations are, to show his willingness to bless our faith!

Jesus created, by some estimates of Bible theologians, between 120 and 180 gallons of the very best wine from H_2O—water. The Word says, not some of the finest wines, but the best of all the others! Which in my humble opinion, sets Jesus' wine apart from every other wine ever made!

If Jesus was willing to accommodate His mother and a wedding party who was unprepared and never even asked, how much more will Jesus be willing to do for you, if you will ask expectantly? **When God sees faith, the bible says God rewards faith**! When God sees our faith and our faith is expectant of Jesus' willingness to help, God rewards our *faith*!

I don't know about you, but I don't serve a God of normal. ***Do you?*** I serve an over the top, Supernatural God of ***more than enough***. The Bible tells us that the day Jesus fed everyone, He multiplied five loaves and two fish to satisfy thousands, and they still had an amazing abundance of leftovers—more than 12 baskets.

God never does anything halfway, He is always giving us His best! Jesus is always advancing our cause! He's **always** doing new things, always going out of His way to be good to us! Always looking for new ways to shine His multiplying ability, His favor-filled atmosphere of blessings, down on His Children!

> Lamentations 3:22-23 NKJV — *Through the Lord's mercies we are not consumed, Because His compassions fail not.* 23 *They are new every morning; Great is Your faithfulness.*

As unbelievable as it seems, God gave us the amazing responsibility of being deciders of how much we expect to receive of His Goodness! Yes, that's right. **We are the deciders, and our only limit to what God wants to do for us is our *faith and expectations of Him*.** Let me repeat the last sentence again— We are the deciders, and our only limit to what God wants to do for us is our faith and expectations of Him. Do you need to read that one more time?

What is your expectation level of God's promises? I mean seriously, how much can you really believe God for? Can you contain your expectations with a gallon bucket? Or do you need a 100 acre reservoir to hold what you're believing God for? Never set your expectations of faith too low. Don't be the one who cheats you out of what God has planned for you. This is why: because we can receive from God as much as we can expect and believe Him for.

Well, Charlie, that's pretty bold! Yes, it is. I'm glad you noticed.

This is exactly how God wants us to approach Him! Because of our relationship with Jesus, we have been justified! God looks at us just as if we were Jesus. He doesn't reward us because of our identity, but because of the identity we receive from Jesus. Jesus is our qualification. He is the reason we can and should walk in identifiable confidence and boldness. When we approach His throne, our flag of faith is held high, *not only with the confidence to ask, but with firm expectations to receive what God is willing to do for us.*

Friend, I must ask you a personal question. **How high is the bar of your faith and level of expectation today? Have you placed it high enough,**

so only God is able to meet such a request? Or can you easily trip over your expectations without any effort?

I don't know about you, but every time I realize and remember what we are talking about here, I want to look around at my circumstances, and raise the bar of my faith and expectation even higher than what I thought was out of reach only a moment ago.

> Jeremiah 33:2-3 — *This is God's Message, the God who made earth, made it livable and lasting, known everywhere as God: 'Call to me and I will answer you. I'll tell you marvelous and wondrous things that you could never figure out on your own.'*

How many of us think we can figure things out on our own most of the time? All of us? Why don't we just be honest with ourselves and admit we are not, and will never (*ouch*) be what we think we are, without Jesus' help and intervention!

This scripture says, God is willing to give us classified information, and wants to reveal amazing things that only He knows. How amazing is this promise for us, for those who have a relationship with Jesus? God wants to outdo Himself, *in ways we can't think or even imagine*, every time we call on Him. This is God's promise, for the 'right now moments' we face each and every day. As long as we trust God for what we need, Jesus will show us what we need to know, exactly in the *right-now moments*.

Today, yes, I said today—and it doesn't matter what society thinks, or what the media has to say—**God has thought long and hard and made detailed plans to show us things, GREAT things, amazing and wonderful things, *if* we are willing to believe, look and listen to his instructions—**things we know nothing about.

On the other hand, the accuser continually tries to convince everyone that this is a terrible time to be alive and things will never get better. And even as the atmosphere is changing for the better right now before our very eyes, the accuser's minions are screaming that this is too good to be true! This is not the new normal of what our expectations should be going forward into the future! And the pleas of the confused and misled continue to cry for the crooked and corrupt path of familiarity they've grown so accustomed to!

Don't be caught up in the moment! Don't be deceived by the cleverly worded political buzzwords of the day! Things change and God changes things for those who pray and seek to change things! One moment of faith changed everything in November 2024! In case you haven't realized lately, this is one of the most amazing and exciting times in all of history.

We need to fully embrace this moment that we are witnessing. These are the good ole days. **This is only the beginning of what's to come. Right now, this very moment in time, what we see happening, is the trajectory God wants for the whole world. Praise God! What we are witnessing is the beginning of Plan A, in real time. Again, Praise God! Fully alive in 2025! Living out loud and proud of Jesus.**

We have been given the ability and the authority to live, write and weave our story into the amazing story of Jesus, which is God's AMAZING story! The story of Jesus, and what God wants to do for everyone who has a relationship **with Him**, is amazing! What a better time to be alive in 2025, or any time in history to be blessed by God.

Jesus is not even slightly distracted or hindered by any of the false messaging being reported by the media! God's favor and goodness, if you'll look through your spiritual glasses, shines brightly, each and every day of the *right now.* **What has happened so far is only a foretaste of what's to come! We haven't experienced all of God's goodness, we've only experienced a fraction of what is on the horizon**. We have, at best, ever so slightly scratched the surface of what is to come!!

Remember, God is always a God of increase! Don't believe me? Let me ask you. Has anything God ever created stopped re-creating and multiplying itself?? No, it hasn't! It's called God's law of seed-time and harvest! I challenge you to name, or find one thing, God created that ever stopped reproducing itself! You will find, not even one time, has God's law of seed-time and harvest failed!

What's the matter? Don't you believe me? Then why not try opening your spiritual eyes to the wonders all around you? Let God rescue you and open your heart to the promised possibilities awaiting those who trust in Him.

It's like this, friend. Have you ever tried to eradicate a dandelion in your yard? At best, you have accomplished a temporary victory. Listen to me. If God cares enough about the dreaded dandelion, to not let what we call a weed be denied its destiny, how much more value do you have to Him? Immensely more value, let me remind you.

So, take a look at yourself and realize the importance of the way you observe yourself! **You are a King's kid, with full rights of an heir, to everything Jesus' death on the cross, already bought for you to have and enjoy.** Start seeing yourself the way God sees you!

Where you are today, is not—*no matter what, it is not*—where you are going to be forever. If you have or are thinking such, stop making agreements, even if you think they're innocent agreements, with anything contrary to God's word and what you have been promised.

Far too many are in the habit of doing exactly that. They take a thought or temptation, and instead of cutting it off or pulling it out by the root immediately, they ponder it.

At first, only revisiting the thought ever so slightly, but unknowingly letting the ticking time-bomb become a mainstream planted seed in their thought pattern. This usually ends up being acted out upon as it grows, ultimately leading to sin. **Listen friends, even innocent agreements, left unchecked and revisited too many times, can take root and grow into problems!** *Above all, you have to protect and safeguard your heart!*

Not safeguarding your heart leads to an endless cycle of rabbit trails, causing us to lose focus and continually distract us from the calling Jesus has placed on our lives! Once the devil has his thumb on the pulse of your heart, your heart is in a weakened state, and always has a hard time recovering.

That's why Jesus told us to trust Him, to protect and guard our hearts! For by doing so, we would be unshakable in our faith and always at peace!

> John 16:31-33 MSG — *Jesus answered them, "Do you finally believe? In fact, you're about to make a run for it— saving your own skins and abandoning me. But I'm not abandoned. The Father is with me. I've told you all this so that trusting me, you will be unshakable and assured, deeply at peace. In this godless world you will continue to experience difficulties. But take heart! I've conquered the world."*

This moment in time is just a stopping off place on your journey. **When you walk in the Favor of God, good things are going to come your way.** And with no other effort except YOU using your faith to believe and receive God's blessing.

Just one moment of God's Favor can excel and propel you. It can take you places you could have never gotten on your own. I tell you this from the voice of experience. Because when I look back on my life, I can't believe all the amazing things God has done and the places God has taken me. And this I know, my success is only by God's amazing grace and His unbelievable favor, propelling me to where I am today, or at any given moment.

Am I tooting my own horn? While it may sound like I am, I want you to know I'm not tooting my horn. But I will blow and sound the alarm of Jesus' horn all day long. And I won't downplay or try to hide anything God has done for me, or any way that Jesus has Blessed me, at His Father's instruction.

And I want you to know, the Trinity (God the Father, Jesus the Son, and the Holy Spirit of God, living in the heart of every Christian) wants the very same thing for you!

This isn't a game like Monopoly! You don't have to wait for your blessings and rewards to pass 'go'! All you have to do is have faith and believe that God willingly desires to bless you, and has already prepared your blessing for you. It's ready for you to step into, sit down at the extravagant feast, and enjoy what has been prepared for you!

Tim Schaffer, a very good friend of mine, patiently taught me what I'm trying to convey to you! I wrote a book about it, called "Parking Lot

Faith" and its premise is simple. When you have enough faith to believe in God for a front row parking spot every time, you have enough faith to pass the test of faith for everything, AKA "Poppy Seed size faith, like Jesus taught about!"

Jesus wanted us to build our faith through small baby steps, so we could grow in belief. As we take those baby steps of faith successfully, He knows that the same amount of faith will ALWAYS be enough, to believe Him for anything. **Jesus doesn't want us to keep taking the same test of Faith over and over and over.** Jesus wants us to realize and build from those experiences, knowing our measure of faith has already been given to us by God, and will always be more than *enough faith* for anything we will ever need or face. No matter what.

How do you walk in God's favor? You walk in God's favor by using the faith God has given to you. ***Here it is again… "You walk in God's favor, by using the parking lot amount of faith God has given to you. Which is always more than enough faith to believe you can do what God's word and promises say you can do."***

You might say, I'm sorry I missed that, but what kind of faith is that again? **Parking Lot Faith!** Yes, I know what you're thinking. At first I had a hard problem with the simplicity of understanding this concept too! But here it is again for you. **Parking Lot Faith is when you pray and have enough faith that there will always be a great front row spot for you, no matter what store you go to, or when/what time of day you go.** Yes, *Parking Lot Faith* is simplistic faith. Yet I believe, like its cousin, the poppyseed, *Parking Lot Faith* is all the faith you will ever need. Simplistic, childlike faith.

Jesus didn't make the concept of faith hard to grasp and we shouldn't either. Remember Jesus said, "there is no more or less faith!" The Bible says everyone has been given a measure of faith! ***Everyone.*** God's plan from the beginning has always been to equip mankind with enough faith to do everything God called us to do—everything He promised us, we can do!

> Jeremiah 29:11-13 NKJV — *For I know the thoughts/plans that I think toward you, says the LORD, thoughts/plans of peace and not of evil, to give you a future and a hope.*

Then you will call upon Me and go and pray to Me, and I will listen to you. And you will seek Me and find Me, when you search for Me with all your heart.

Again, **God has great plans for us—*for all of us who believe*** and are favor-minded. Does this excite you? Okay, I'll say it again, ***"God has great plans for everyone who will believe and accept his favor for them."*** Does God's plan excite you?

Fantastic Plans, Brilliant Plans, Accelerating Plans which lay ahead of us, not behind us. Plans so great that if we were to know the extent and dimensions of God's plans for us, even a fraction of the knowledge would be, and is unbelievably, beyond our comprehension!

I don't know about you, but I know God's plans are immensely bigger and better than my plans ever have been, or will ever be! How do I know? How do I know? I thought you'd never ask, but I'm glad you did. Because of my personal relationship and experience with Jesus. It's all because Jesus Loves me!

Yes, I'm bragging about the fact that Jesus loves me. Jesus... Loves... Me! As you too, friends, should be bragging about the same realization of exactly how much you are loved. I have made John's connection and realization as we read in the book of John about the one, whom Jesus loved. I have come to realize... I'm the one, yes, I'm the one! And so you will be, friends, when you come to the same realization of how much Jesus loves you.

I have experienced the Goodness of God, because I have experienced God's plans, in real time. And every time my so-called plans have been compared to God's plans, I've realized, my plans were so insignificantly small compared to the larger than life plans God had. He amazingly brings them to fruition, right in front of my very own eyes.

God's plans know no limits whatsoever! **God's plans know no limits whatsoever. *And* the amazing attribute about God's plans are, He never stops wanting you and I to be part of His plans!** Brilliant plans God has thought about, in great detail. Amazing plans God has crafted and worked to perfection, for our behalf!

Sadly, so many people, even Christians, never choose to completely go along with God's plans. They may know they should go along with God's plans, but somehow, they can't seem to give up control of their poorly, flawed plans built out of their worn out self effort. **Therefore, consistently missing out on God's amazing willingness, to be good to them.**

When the Lord goes to the trouble to get someone a word, through an evangelist, author, pastor, singer or anyone telling them how God wants to work in their life, **how** good God is, and **how** Jesus wants to meet their needs, **immediately**, the devil's pawn rises getting busy doing everything he can to steal the blessing God has for His intended **recipients. The devil never wants our hearts to be encouraged.**

We must never make any agreements with our own thoughts or ambitions, with the accuser or anyone else, when the agreements are going to diminish the Power of God being released, or spoken into our lives. That's worth reading again, friend.

The devil, above everyone else, knows the commanding power of receiving, and the tremendous value of applying a God given word to someone's heart and life at exactly the right time! It's no wonder so many pastors, evangelists, Christian authors, and speakers are constantly having their character questioned and being subjected to endless and unscrupulous attacks by the devil's social media and propaganda machine!

Always with one purpose in mind! So, the condemning results of the attack will cause as many people as possible, including Christians, to hear the word, and hear it, and hear it, but never let it take root and grow in their heart or in their lives!

Take notice, friend! When you see such incidents of attack happening on social media platforms, realize, and know the man or woman of God under attack has been called, is highly Favored and Loved by the Lord and the devil knows it! They are a huge threat to the devil's unending plans of demise, or the devil wouldn't be working so hard to silence them!! Jesus faced the same method of attack from the Pharisee's in His day!

A good gardener never stops trying to cultivate the seeds he has planted, into thriving growing plants that produce. A good gardener's motivation is always the same thing, the harvest. **It's always about the harvest.**

> James 1:19-24 MSG — *Heed this warning friend. Post this at all the intersections, dear friends: Lead with your ears, follow up with your tongue, and let anger straggle along in the rear. God's righteousness doesn't grow from human anger. So throw all spoiled virtue and cancerous evil in the garbage. In simple humility, let our gardener, God, landscape you with the Word, making a salvation-garden of your life. 22-24. Don't fool yourself into thinking that you are a listener when you are anything but, letting the Word go in one ear and out the other. Act on what you hear! Those who hear and don't act are like those who glance in the mirror, walk away, and two minutes later have no idea who they are, or what they look like.*

"So throw all spoiled virtue and cancerous evil in the garbage. In simple humility, let our gardener, God, landscape you with the Word, making a salvation-garden of your life."

God's intentions and hopes for every human being, is for them to be good and receptive soil! Soil for His word to seed, sprout, grow, be cultivated, and brought to fruition in our lives. I pray, "God, help all of Your children to be good soil and let their hearts become a salvation garden and produce, yes, produce and never stop producing fruit to be harvested!"

We hear and see, from time to time, the percent of people living below the poverty line in America and around the world. **We are both moved and appalled by the magnitude of it!** Something even more alarming and detrimental is the percentage of Christians living below the spiritual poverty line. When it comes to receiving and enjoying the abundant life, God has promised to all who will believe in the word! This form of poverty should really bother us, but does it? Well?

Why is it, that so many of God's children never live even close to the spiritual level of relationship and life God has planned, and that they

are entitled to? The Bible says, "The poor you will always have among you." What is your definition of poor?

There is poor, financially speaking of course, but there is also poor spiritually speaking as well! Poor is a frame of mind, a mindset and lifestyle that God never intended "His Children" to live in. God gets no glory by someone being poor. Physically, mentally, spiritually, financially, or any other description of the poor in life you want to use.

How can any of us expect to have a thriving spiritual life, if we're not constantly cultivating our own relationship with Jesus living in our heart, willing to help us? This includes the others around us as well, to the absolute best of our ability and the way God has laid out for us, to disciple others.

> John 10:10 NKJV — *The thief does not come except to steal, and to kill, and to destroy. I have come that they may have life, and that they may have it more abundantly.* [Note: I love this verse and use it often. I love what it says, but also the promise it makes, of the best kind of life imaginable!]

If you will ***accept and embrace*** the life Jesus has given to you, let me tell you friend, God has greater levels of His favor and blessing in store for you. Levels you can't even begin to comprehend, and no level unattainable! It's up to us and how much each one of us wants to believe in God for our lives!

I challenge you,* Dare to dream bigger than your efforts will bring to the table. Dare to keep your focus continuously on cultivating the God-sized vision, the Holy Spirit has placed in front of you.** Be daring enough, to make God your partner. Be daring enough to embrace God's willingness to help you and make your plans large, so large, there's no way possible you could ever accomplish what you're wanting to do by yourself. ***And then, get into the position of faith, to receive what you have asked for.

If you haven't asked God to help you achieve your dreams and help plan your life, *what are you waiting for?* Seriously!

Those things are part of your spiritual bill of rights…your God given rights. Those truth's are a part of your ***spiritual inheritance,*** and they have been available to you from the first day you accepted Jesus as your Lord and Saviour!

> Deuteronomy 32:46-47 GW — *He said to them, Pay attention to all these warnings I've given you today. Then you will command your children to faithfully obey every word of these teachings. Don't think these words are idle talk. They are your life!*

A while back I read of a man named George Stansberry, who told a group of Bible college students, "If you leave this building today and see a needy person on the street and give him a dollar, you showed him unmerited favor. He did nothing to deserve it. But if you leave here and find that same man breaking into your car to steal your radio, and you give him a dollar, that is grace, because that is the opposite of what he deserves."

God gives us so many good things. And the things God gives us, we must realize, are all undeserved.

From salvation and grace, to His love and forgiveness, along with the blessings of His constant favor and willingness to give us all those things, unconditionally. **God wants you to learn to cultivate them, to walk in them, to constantly expect them and run with them, to inhabit them and soak what you have been given up like a sponge.**

You have been given the ability to grow all of God's blessings to a ripened harvest, in your salvation garden! And then—*this is the most important part*—give them away. Give them away? Yes, give them away like there's no tomorrow!

Give them away, without fear of ever having enough to share each day. Give as often and as much as you want! Realize and believe you have provision enough today to share, and tomorrow you'll have the same.

You have my word, but more importantly you have God's Word that you will. So, you will. *I know from personal experience, you will!*

This is the plan God has for everyone who is willing—willing to believe and to receive His goodness. If you are willing to do what I've asked you to do, I've one more piece of advice for you. **Put on your spiritual**

seat belt and buckle up, because nobody knows how to work His plan for your life like God does.

And speaking of plans—we're going to talk a little bit more about it in the next chapter. I hope you're looking forward to the conversation, as much as I am. I just love it when a *good plan* comes together!

CHAPTER 6

IS GOD'S PLAN, YOUR PLAN?

Don't you just love a good story? Here's one I heard tell of sometime back. It's a story about a hero of mine, and one I think you'll find common ground with. Let's take a moment and read it together.

In the opening pages of his autobiography, *An American Life*, Ronald Reagan writes, I was raised to believe that God had a plan for everyone and that seemingly random twists of fate are all a part of His plan. My mother, a small woman with auburn hair and a sense of optimism that ran as deep as the cosmos, told me, everything in life happened for a purpose.

She said all things were part of God's plan, even the most disheartening setbacks, and in the end, everything worked out for the best. If something went wrong, she said, you didn't let it get you down: You stepped away from it, stepped over it, and moved on.

Later on, she added, something good will happen and you'll find yourself thinking - "If I hadn't had that problem back then, this better thing that did happen, wouldn't have happened to me." Although I lost the job at *Montgomery Ward*, I left home again in search of work. Although I didn't know it then, I was beginning a journey that would take me a long way from Dixon and fulfill all my dreams and then some.

My mother, as usual, was right.... SOURCE: *An American Life* by Ronald Reagan

Jesus had a way of both telling and writing a story at the same time! The Bible calls them parables. Parable - A parable is a short and simple story that teaches a religious or moral lesson.

I think Jesus really told parables, to help us remember and keep us on track! And to always bring us back to the realization, Plan B, would always be designed to bring us back to *Plan A*. I suppose you could use every other letter in the alphabet as well, describing God's desire for *Plan A* to be accomplished in our lives.

Plan A — believe, receive, and live the abundant life that God has always had planned for us! All other plans, work together for them that love the Lord, and are called to his purpose — to bring about Plan A. Here's what I think is a great question for you. Can you tell me why, our human nature has such a hard time just going with Plan A—which is God's plan—and sticking to the plan?

> Mark 4:39-41 MSG — *Awake now, he told the wind to pipe down and said to the sea, "Quiet! Settle down!" The wind ran out of breath; the sea became smooth as glass. Jesus reprimanded the disciples: "Why are you such cowards? Don't you have any faith at all?" 41 They were in absolute awe, staggered. "Who is this, anyway?" they asked. "Wind and sea at his beck and call!"*

Why do we love everything new we acquire, except for change? New furniture? Love it! New car? Love it! New guitar? Love, love, love it! But **change**? Yes, change, as in, from ordinary to extraordinary! Friend, I'm talking about something different than the norm. And since we are friends now, I feel from one friend to another, it's my obligation to tell you.

The change I'm talking about, is something completely different from the mediocrity most people have become comfortable and are used to living with. Something so far beyond anything we could ever hope or imagine. **Something so much better God's got for us, something totally different than we've ever experienced.**

I could continue to tell you what we're getting ready to experience, will be so good for you that you can't even imagine. I could also tell you the one who is getting ready to deliver this amazing life changing event, has been preparing for this moment since the beginning of time. **But**, if we're going to keep waiting, hesitating and clinging to the mediocrity of familiarity—and failing to open ourselves up to the possibilities of what's been prepared for us—why would I bother to continue to talk about it?

Aren't you glad God's not that way? God has instructed the Holy Spirit to court you. And He intends for Jesus to keep taking you and I to the "abundant life dance!" Providing and giving you and me with unlimited opportunities to dance and be blessed, whether we choose to accept the invitation, or not!

Does anyone ever remember, when your father, brother, or someone who was capable of removing your training wheels from your bicycle, removed them? I can remember my training wheels being removed from my bicycle. I can remember being fearful when I rode, and took off, that I would fall over and crash! But much to my surprise, I didn't crash!

I didn't crash, instead I took off and rode my bike amazingly well. I even learned how to ride wheelies, backwards and to jump over ramps like Evel Knievel! I have been riding ever since. Even when years have lapsed in between rides, I still ride amazingly well! Thus, I believe the term was coined. It's just like riding a bicycle, once you learn, you never forget! And you always have the ability at your disposal, anytime you need to use it!

Why can't our spiritual lessons Jesus teaches about faith, be more like that? **Isn't that how it should be with our faith Building experiences, when Jesus helps us through our need?** Shouldn't we be able to relate to what we've learned, take off our faith training wheels and be able to reuse that knowledge, at any given time? The answer is yes, we should! Jesus expects us to do exactly that. Jesus expects us and wants us to continuously ride wheelies of our faith, like a surfer rides big waves.

When Jesus helps us through life's circumstances, and we use our limited *Training Wheels of Faith*, we believe Jesus will help us. If it was indeed enough Faith, to pass the test and get through the trial, victoriously, shouldn't we remember that it's just like riding a bike? If Jesus helped us pass the test of faith by removing our training wheels and being victorious before, shouldn't we be able to draw on our experience and (take them off for good) trust Jesus and our relationship every time another test appears? ***Again, the answer is, "yes!"***

God will never ask you to do something, or to go through something without making sure the provision will always be there—before you will ever need it. *Yes, you need to say it aloud and get used to saying the word, "provision."*

When things start to change, and sometimes they will change quickly, God wants you to be prepared with the measure of faith/readiness He has given to you and always realize your Faith will *always* be more than enough and all you will ever need, *no matter what. No matter what!?* *YES, NO MATTER WHAT!*

Now, while it's not hard to believe, Jesus had the amazing ability to accomplish all the miracles He did. Far too many in the church have a hard time believing that *we have the authority to do the same, and even greater miracles still today.* Yet we do. We have been given the authority to not only try, but to succeed! Have you ever tried to attempt something like Jesus did? Why not?

I remember hearing the story about my pastor, J.L. Schaffer. One summer's afternoon, he bravely spoke to a thunderstorm, during a church building process, and it listened! The cement masons were right in the middle of pouring the entire foundation and floor on a new church, which they were in the process of building. Everything was going according to schedule, when suddenly a cool breeze rolled in.

All who were working that day began to worry, as they saw the black clouds quickly forming. **"Oh my goodness," everyone sighed, quickly sensing and smelling the atmosphere changing.** The winds roared and leaves curled with anticipation. Everyone on the ground that day realized they were facing the real possibility of a calamity and all their work ruined. With the possibility of costing hundreds of thousands of dollars to redo.

What Pastor Schaffer did next still amazes me, and I believe is pretty close to the equivalent of what Moses did by faith, when he held up his rod and split the Red Sea. Without saying a word, Pastor Schaffer got in his car, picked up his Bible and went to the edge of the property. **He held up his Bible to his face and he spoke to that storm,** just like Jesus did after the disciples awakened Him on the storm at sea. That fierce storm, to the surprise of everyone present, split in the middle and went around them!

It was an amazing testimony of Pastor Schaffer's faith, and God's willingness to acknowledge his expectations of faith. A simple and tremendous miracle, not to be forgotten! Not one single drop of water touched the church property, or any of the wet concrete, that day! Pastor Schaffer didn't do it, but his faith in the God of all possibilities did.

How much faith did he have? Enough. That's how much. **How much faith is required to move the hand of God?** A speck of faith. Each of us, God has equipped to do the same as what Pastor Schaffer did that day. How many events greater than that are awaiting your arrival and moment of faith?

What is possible when one person is willing to believe and take God at His word? Everything is possible, to him who believes. Self-effort never builds your faith! *Only when you cast your complete dependence and care on Jesus, to provide what you're looking for,* does your faith have an opportunity to *deliver what you're looking for, and grow!*

How much do you want from God and how much do you want of God? The answer always is, **"How much can you believe God wants to be good to you?"**

At what point in our faith/walk and relationship with Jesus, do we wholeheartedly believe and receive God's plan as our plan? For every promise, God has instructed His Son Jesus to lavishly deliver and distribute to whosoever will Believe. Jesus stands ready, having done His part! God has done His Part! The Holy Spirit is ready to move! Now has come the time, for every one, who claims to be a believer, to do their part.

What is your part? You know very well what your part is! Your part is not to deliver the results of what you're looking for, but only believe that what you're looking for is possible, and that God willingly wants to do it.

God has always loved us and never has stopped loving us! God has continued to give and has never stopped giving. Again, I say decision time has come! **How much** can you believe to receive, of Jesus and His Father, through the Power of The Holy Spirit? He has already, both sacrificially and willingly, given you the chance to receive.

The time has come... to believe and also receive ALL of it—every last syllable of every promise God has ever made to you. To fully embrace and use, to the best of your ability, what Jesus sacrificed His life for, so you could have everything God has Planned for you.

Romans 1:18-36 talks about the fact that there are so many chances a person will hear and have a chance to come to the gospel, and in relationship with Jesus! After that, eventually their hearts will become so hardened, they will completely ignore the truth and pursue sin without any remorse.

The Bible says, God desires that no one should perish. But eventually a person's heart will become so hardened by sin, they will never come to salvation. **Why would anyone ever want to take the chance of missing Heaven and ending up in Hell?**

That is why we need to be doing everything we can do to bring someone into a relationship with Jesus. To tell them, and help them realize the good news. To show them, leading by example, what is possible and attainable, by having a relationship with Jesus. **To let them know an amazingly blessed and powerful life awaits their arrival.** When they believe, and receive, everything possible that Jesus wants to give them.

What does *everything* entail? *Everything* means even unbelievable things—thing that you can't imagine. It means things even greater than the scripture reveals about Peter, which I'm getting ready to share with you! Are you ready? Ready to fasten your seatbelt and hang on? Because **we're getting ready to go beyond the comfort level of anything you think is possible—*again!***

> Acts 5:12-16 MSG — *(the power of the Holy Spirit that is available to every believer, is amazing) Through the work of the apostles, many God-signs were set up among the people, many wonderful things done. They all met regularly and in remarkable harmony on the Temple porch named after Solomon. But even though people admired them a lot,*

outsiders were wary about joining them. On the other hand, those who put their trust in the Master were added right and left, men and women both. They even carried the sick out into the streets and laid them on stretchers and bedrolls, hoping they would be touched by Peter's shadow when he walked by.

They came from the villages surrounding Jerusalem, throngs (which means too many to count) of them, bringing the sick and bedeviled, and they all were healed! **They were all what? Seriously? I just read what Luke wrote, didn't I? They were *all* Healed! Not by the hem of Jesus' garment, but by the *shadow* of a disciple and believer of Jesus!**

I'm not trying to be too over the top here. But I want to make a big deal, **no, I want to make a *huge* deal out of what happened that day!** I want to reiterate, not *some* of them were healed, but every single one of them. All of them. That means, **all of them!** Not 98 out of a 100, not 99.9 percent, but 100 out of 100 were healed!

They were **impossibly** healed, by the shadow of someone who—*this is the moment for you to realize, you've been given the same authority by Jesus, to insert your name here*—took Jesus at His Word, and **believed, and used what Jesus gave them and told them what was possible if they were to use what they had been given!**

Do you suppose, any of those who were healed, had mountain high faith? Or do you suppose it was mustard size faith capable of moving their mountains? What do you think? More importantly, what kind of faith do you think Peter had? **Sometimes, I think we give more credit to the human nature and abilities someone else has.**

I believe if we were to measure the amount of faith Peter had, we would find it to be the same amount God gave us. And that the amount was just enough. Not more than enough, not less than enough, but exactly the right amount. The mustard size seed—a tiny amount required to move the hand of God.

Let me remind us all, what kind of faith does the Bible say is required? *All that is required is a seed of faith.* A mustard seed size amount of faith. Which, like I said, is pulled from and supplied by the more than adequate measure of faith God has already given to all of us, including you, my dear friend. **We can turn our world on its head**, just like the disciples did. We just need to do one thing. **Believe everything is possible**. Believe everything the Bible promises, which the word of God has delivered from the cross, through the resurrection and victory over death by Jesus'!

And it is already in our access—at our disposal to use! We don't have to wait for anything. We have already been well equipped **to win and achieve victory.** We must never forget, Jesus, our Saviour is alive and seated next to his father, making intercession continually for those who are in relationship with him!

Jesus' triumphant resurrection is the reason why we can stand up, proclaim and receive every promise God has made to us, and do the impossible!

God, even after all this time, is still doing new miracles all around us... day after day after day. He is doing new, new, new things. God is, and has always been, a God of *new*. New mercies every day. New amounts of grace given to us every day. New moments of forgiveness, when we come with a repentant heart, every day. New amounts of God's dispersed blessings everyday. Along with every promise eagerly awaiting our arrival.

God is not bound by yesterday! God is still in the business of doing something new, if we only believe and are willing to receive what He wants to do, and is doing. If you want to see the new that God longs for and desires to do in your life and give you, then I suggest you start believing and grabbing hold of God's Amazing Plans. Grab hold of them and "Run Towards The Light" like you are not responsible for delivering any of the results. Because *you're not!* Again, I reiterate because it's important, you are not, and will never be, responsible for the results you're seeking from God! You are only responsible for the recognizable amount of Faith it takes to be noticed!

How powerful is God's ability to detect our faith? Would a comparison to our vision and the human eye's ability to see, be a fair comparison? I think you can see by what you're going to read next, how detectable, even a slight flicker of our faith is to God, when He sees it.

The Human Eye is Incredibly powerful. It contains more than 100 million light-sensitive cells and some of the fastest muscles in our bodies. It can distinguish about 500 shades of gray, and in very dim light retinal rod cells are sensitive enough to detect a candle flame 30 miles away. [SOURCE: sciencefocus.com , thedonutwhole.com]

God is about uniting His people and their faith together like never before! He is about to do something new, I believe, that no one has ever witnessed! **Isn't it time we all unite our faith together and completely embrace what God has been waiting and ready to do from the beginning?**

Don't be a *doubting Thomas*, the one who misses the opportunity to jump on the relationship level-up bus! It's time to come out from under the bus of condemnation and unbelief, and get on the relationship level-up bus! To pursue continually and seek God as to what your part is going to be, in the greatest quest and adventure ever known to mankind! It's time to step up and into a brand new level of commitment and relationship with Jesus. The scandalous "mustard size faith" belief produces a faith that causes amazing things to happen! And guess what, friend? Believing God's promises in faith, without fail, still delivers the same amazing results today and everyday!

If you ever want to experience the *Goodness of God* and the *Peace that passes all understanding* that the Bible talks about, you have to get comfortable with the direction God is taking you—no matter what the direction or plan God has for you. You must make this incredible realization: "As long as God knows the plan for my life, that's all I need to know!" **At some point, we all need to make the irrevocable decision to completely trust God in every area of life, no matter what!** I believe if Jesus were writing this, He would think that right now is the perfect time for a story. What do you think?

> One day a boy and his father were sitting on the back porch, enjoying the shade and a cup of iced tea, and taking a break from their Saturday chores. Thinking about his cool swimming hole, suddenly the boy broke the silence. He asked his father, "Dad, if three frogs were sitting on a limb that hung over a pool, and one frog decided to jump off, into the pool, how many frogs would be left on the limb?"

The dad looked up from his tea, struck by the simplicity of the questions. Meeting the boys eye, he stated simply, "Two."

"No," the son replied. After a brief pause, and his father's questioning look he restated, "There are three frogs on the limb. One decides to jump into the pool. How many are on the limb now?"

The dad smiled back a response thinking he understood the wit of his son, "Oh, I get it. If one decides to jump, the others would follow too. So there are none left... right?"

Shaking his head slowly, the boy said, "No dad, the answer is three. There are still three frogs on the limb. One frog only *decided* to jump. He didn't actually take any action to make it happen!"

We can hear how God is wanting to do something new, and we can act like we want to be involved. We can even see and be convinced that the impossible could actually happen! But, **until we decide to jump into whatever God has planned**, and make the commitment to be involved, **we will never have a part in the miracle of what God has planned for us**—a miracle Jesus is waiting to deliver!

One of my favorite scriptures, Jeremiah 29:11, tells us that God knows the plans He has—plans He has always had—for you to prosper and bring about your best life now! What does your best life now look like?

I'm not quite sure... But the word of God tells us this description in the book of Ephesians: "Your best life now, looks like something larger, wider, higher and deeper, than you could ever dream, in your wildest imagination!"

Some might say, "Charlie, what are you trying to be, a motivational speaker, life coach, or something?" Well, I can think of a lot worse things I have been accused of, than being a faith motivator and cheerleader for Jesus! What I'm trying to help us do, is realize exactly what we have been given, and how well **God has equipped each and every one of us to do what we've been called to do.** To somehow point you to the greatest Saviour, Creator, story teller, motivational speaker, cheerleader, and life coach that ever walked God's green earth! And His name is Jesus!

It's all of our jobs—hear yourself saying, "It's my job,"—to lift up Jesus so all may be drawn unto Him. I think pastors and those in pastoral leadership, should be more motivational and uplifting from their pulpits too. Lord knows, no one will hear the encouragement they need from the world's news or social media.

The Bible says, we are snared by the words of our mouths and one day **we all will be held accountable for the words encouraging or discouraging that we have spoken.** Especially those who have been charged with the responsibility of influencing others from their pulpits.

Why not take this moment of opportunity to get alone with God in your prayer closet, and seek God as to what we have just talked about, and what He has for your life. **I challenge you to not only ask, but use your faith to wholeheartedly believe as you ask.** To ardently seek, getting into the position and with expectation to receive, what God has for you—*what God wants to give to you*.

I want to leave this chapter challenging you to pursue your relationship with God the Father, the Holy Spirit, and Jesus, like never before! Take time each and every day to pray and ask above all else, for kingdom plans to be revealed to you, in vivid color! And for God, Jesus and the Holy Spirit to help you make every detailed plan they have for you, become your plan!

What do you think God has in store for you? **Why not make the choice, in advance, to say yes, No matter what it is?** Sounds like a good plan to me. How about you?

CHAPTER 7

RECEIVE YOUR CALLING

What is your calling? What has God called you to do? Have you asked God what His plan and will is for your life? Are you listening for and willing to heed His voice? Or are you running from what God has called you to do? Is this a Jonah moment for you, or an Isaiah moment?

My mother, God rest her soul, always wanted me to grow up to be a pastor. And although **I felt her prayers trying to be answered by the prompting of the Holy Spirit many times,** I always found an excuse and a reason to put off her wishes, ultimately saying "No" to what she wanted for me.

My excuses ranged from my circumstances at any given time, job, financial situation, wants, needs, ambitions, starting a business, later running a business, etcetera. I could go on, and you might be thinking to yourself as you're reading, "I can relate to what he's saying!"

Finally, at 45 years of age, after J.L. Schaffer, the original pastor in my church, passed away. And the interim pastor of three years moved on to other work, where God had called him. And I felt the call of God to step up! I had ministered filling the pulpit several times. But **this time, even though I was thinking only short term, it felt different.** I volunteered to be the interim pastor for a couple weeks or so, filling in again, while we found another pastor.

While that may seem small to someone else, I remember thinking, oh my goodness, what had I done? While you may be chuckling, believe me, the temporary agreement I made with God, was a big step of faith for me! I think and believe for most Christians, that when they make a commitment in pursuing God's will, **the first, 100% committed yes of your true calling, is ALWAYS the hardest.**

I believe what saying "Yes" did for me (after getting over the initial hurdle of fear), was to open a door of faith and opportunity, which God had already prepared for me and was awaiting my arrival. In the weeks following my, "Yes," and my first sermon, titled: *Let's Make A Deal!* (Ha ha), the call of God became more apparent with each day that passed.

I remember trying to call around and find good recommendations from other pastors. Call after call would hit wall after wall. Even then, I continued to be optimistic and hopeful to help find a good candidate to fill our need, who could become our new pastor. Until one day, in a moment, everything changed. I made a phone call to Pastor Bill Mickler. He was a pastor friend I had met many years before. Bill patiently listened to my plea for help in finding a replacement. As we talked, I remember the beginning of a feeling in my spirit, as though he might actually know someone he would recommend!

I was encouraged, until he abruptly interrupted our conversation and stopped me cold. **He said, "Charlie,... I'm not going to help you."** *Not going to help me?* I couldn't believe what I had heard. He could easily tell I was in wonder as to why he would say such a thing.

Then he confidently and calmly said, "The reason I'm not going to help you is, "God has just told me, you are the one God wants. You are the replacement, the one God wants to use to fill the position you're looking to fill! And **I believe God's telling me,** *you've known this for a while now."*

After a few moments of silence, I said, "Hello? Hello, is this connection good? Are you there? Hello, hello?" hoping that somehow, he had misspoke. But knowing instead, God had miraculously spoken a confirming word through him to me—and he was right! We graciously talked for a while and then **he prayed for me and asked God to use me, in a way that would bless and touch many lives.** I still remember that moment, sitting there feeling humbled, but honored, scared, but empowered!

At that moment, I knew somewhere in Heaven, my mother was smiling proudly!

That my friends, was 16 years ago. Hundreds of sermons, five books later and this being the sixth book God has prompted me to write. Even though, after the first book, I said, I would never do that again... Ha ha, never say never! I say all of those things, not to brag on myself, but to brag on what God can do with a simple, YES!

What is God calling you to? Not what are you doing, but what you think God has called you to do! This is a very serious question, that all Christians should want to continually pursue and know! Yes, like you, there have been numerous times that I have questioned God about things that happened in life. Things I could not figure out or understand. But each time, when God has called me to do something, after praying and even sometimes like Jonah, having a wrestling match with myself about it, I have said yes! And here we are today, having this conversation about your calling.

I feel as though I must remind you of someone who loves you, and is still praying for you and your calling. Now that you've heard my story, I must ask again. What is your calling? What has God called you to do? **Are you listening and willing? Or are you running and wrestling with yourself about what God has called you to do?** In order to receive your true calling from God, I believe you have to **break off every agreement you have ever made with anyone and everyone**, including the devil, who might have a contrary opinion about your calling and what the word of God says. Agreements with the accuser, agreements with daily temptations, agreements with people around you, agreements within yourself and with anything else that will ever keep you from doing what's right, and your calling!

Even innocent little agreements, if revisited or left unchecked, can lead to detrimental alliances and acts of sin. Sometimes breaking an agreement before it becomes a stronghold is easy. Sometimes it takes a lot of repetition. We must take our thoughts captive, and continually break them off of us, moment by moment, until they are completely eliminated!

The more you get used to breaking agreements in their infancy, the easier you realize it is, before they become life altering events and derailing issues of the heart. I'm of the firm belief that there is not just one calling on a person's life in the relationship they have with Jesus, there are many, many, many callings. I also believe, with each calling, one should pray ardently, to know that the prompting is truly by the Holy Spirit calling them, and not their own desires.

Many people have pursued personal callings of what they thought was God given, but to later find it wasn't. And through no fault of Gods, have been thoroughly hurt and disappointed in the process! Ultimately blaming and holding God responsible, for their failure. **A true calling or vision from God, for whatever the task might be, is without repentance** and ultimately with faith and prayer if pursued, will always have more than enough provisions provided by God, to always see the vision and calling come to fruition. No matter what it is, how big it is, or how much it costs.

According to the Website, *answers.com*, the word *called* appears 625 times in the Bible. Jesus called the disciples and immediately—yes, ***immediately*** they threw down their nets, stopped fishing, and followed Jesus. They didn't bother to consider their lives, their family's lives, their livelihoods, or what they might have to give up. **They immediately dropped everything and followed Jesus!** They didn't consider their needs, but yet every need, every want, was miraculously supplied! Even in Matthew 10, when Jesus sent the disciples out to evangelize the countryside, He sent them out with only the shirt on their back, and told them not to worry!

Would you be willing to do what the disciples did, if God called you to such a task? If He told you to go right now, with nothing more than the clothes you have on, and the cash you have in your pocket? Not with the credit card you have in your wallet, because that would not require much Faith! **What do you think would happen to you? Would you sink or swim?**

Do you know what happened to the disciples? Did they all go hungry, have to get crummy jobs, and be forced to stay in homeless shelters? NOPE! Miraculously, every need they had was met! EVERY NEED! Does anyone remember the movie Forrest Gump? Especially the scene when Forrest Gump saw Lt. Dan on the dock?

Forrest jumped off his fishing boat, at full speed, without a care in the world, and swam immediately towards Lt. Dan. He was completely oblivious as to what might happen to him, or his boat. And a few minutes later, his boat crashed into the dock next to where he was standing and came to a screeching halt! Shouldn't we be more like Forrest Gump, without so much concern for our needs and our wants, when Jesus calls us to come and follow Him as well.

Truthfully, if it is God who is really calling us, is there anything we should fear as long as God is for us? If we can trust God with everything else, except what He's calling us to. Don't you think we can confidently and surely *trust God, with everything he is calling us to?*

Again dear reader, if you are a child of God, how are you pursuing your calling, which God has called you to? Have you let go of the steering wheel and jumped off the boat of your own desires? Or are you still trying to drive your boat of desire with one hand, and serve God with the other? Accomplishing more of what you want than what God wants, desires, and longs to give.

Have you asked Jesus to take the wheel? Have you asked Jesus to be your moral compass and direction for your life? While you might think these are pointed questions, personally, I don't think it hurts to ask anyone any of these accountability questions. How about you?

Every calling needs direction! Every mission needs a plan! If you read the story of Jonah, you know Jonah was called. But Jonah refused to go where God called him, and went in the wrong direction of his calling! Many of God's children have indeed experienced Jonah's dilemma, but are somewhat reluctant to admit they have!

Truly, by the words Jesus spoke with *The Great Commission and Charge,* simply put, Jesus has commissioned all of God's sons and daughters! *It's not a matter of if you have been called, but what are you doing with your calling?*

> Genesis 28:15 NIV — *I am with you and will watch over you wherever you go, and I will bring you back to this land. I will not leave you until I have done what I have promised you.*

Wow! This is like A Holy Ghost, EMT, and CPR declaration. **This word** is life giving resuscitation for your journey, anytime you need refreshment for your soul! Isn't this promise amazing?

When you need a scripture to stand on, this scripture has already stood the test of every battle, and comes out victorious every time! This promise exudes CONFIDENCE!!

Confidently, yes, you can walk confidently into the calling you have been given, and hopefully have chosen to receive! Because, no matter what you may be facing, no matter what trial you may be going through, and no matter what things look like, at any given moment, **God always has a plan to bring you back and to turn things around in your favor!** It doesn't matter who you are, where you've been, what you've done, what you've witnessed, or what someone else has done to you!

God never quits working His plans for your life. Like the worship song says, "He never stops working!" Say this aloud? *"**God never quits working his plan or promises in my life!**"* This is a life-changing declaration! Say it again, but this time declare is as if you ***own your faith and the realization of your declaration!***

Do you believe the above statement? Are you sure? You should! I recommend you put this on your fridge, on your bathroom mirror, hang it from the rear view mirror in your car, or anywhere you can see it throughout your day.

Maybe you think, "I'm too far gone!" Really? Or, "I've made too many mistakes!" Says who? "You don't know what I've done!" No, I don't know what you have done, but **let me remind you that you are not on trial here.** Do you think what you've done is bigger than what Jesus can forgive? Listen friend, **there is no sin or circumstance too far from the reach and calling God has placed on someone's life.**

> Luke 23:39-43 MSG — *One of the criminals hanging alongside [Jesus] cursed him: "Some Messiah you are! Save yourself! Save us!" 40-41. But the other one made him shut up: "Have you no fear of God? You're getting the same as him. We deserve this, but not him, he did nothing to deserve this." Then he said, "Jesus, remember me when you*

enter your kingdom." And Jesus said, "Don't worry, I will. Today you will join me in paradise."

This gives all of us such great hope! Don't worry, son. Don't worry, daughter. In other words, "Don't worry, child of God, today you have received the reward of your calling."

Remember when Jesus told the story of the vineyard workers? Amazingly, even those workers, who were called late in the day to work in the vineyard, still received the same benefit and amount of pay as those who were called early in the day.

I imagine, the man's entire life could probably have been so much easier than the life he chose to live. (I think we could all say that. How about you? Come on now!) And no doubt, he probably had several opportunities to do right, before the last one Jesus gave him. Can your relate? In the end, God worked all the things he had done, good, bad and even the ugly together. Somehow, good came out in the end, when this man asked for forgiveness, cast his love for Jesus, and received his calling and reward!

By the way, I suspect Jesus called both of those men to repentance, but only one listened. Don't be like the one who didn't listen. Don't let your heart get so hard that you ignore the calling of the Holy Spirit! From our perception, what we see may be confusing and chaotic. But, in God's realm of the supernatural, it's not that way. God always has everything under control. **God is continually working behind the scenes—working for your good—when you are walking in your calling.**

Are you a believer in Jesus? Do you love Him? Are you seeking God's will for your life? Then you are called according to His purpose! Will there be some wrong turns along the way? You know there will! Probably even multiple U-turns along the way! Seemingly, too many impossible doors to open as well, by God's design. Other doors will close for your protection, and for no other reason, than to show His amazing love for you! Jesus' supernatural goodness, willingness and favor, has already qualified you with absolutely every qualification needed to open endless opportunities, when nothing else would have ever been able to open them at all! If you have been praying about a certain situation that hasn't happened yet, don't give up! Continue to praise God, hang on to your calling, and keep the faith. The light at the end of the tunnel is so much closer than you think. Keep Running! **Run towards the light, as though your need has already been delivered.** That's how faith works. Faith is calling it as though it has already happened, even though it has yet to happen. Faith is thanking God for what is going to happen in advance.

Faith is believing God is busy in real time, orchestrating the right people and right circumstances to come across your path, to bring about what you are believing. Say this aloud with boldness, being aware of each phrase as you hear it, because your relationship with Jesus gives you authority: **"There is nothing... too hard for God... when it comes to God working... His plan... for my life!"**

BUT, I'm too young! But, I'm too old! But, I am too this, or too that... blah, blah. Are you **breathing?** Well? Anytime you say "I'm too—" anything, it is the opposite of faith and what you have been called to receive. What you're really saying is, "But, God, I really don't believe it." I absolutely love what God gave us as a definition of His willingness to help us:

> Ephesians 3:20 MSG — *God can do anything, you know far more than you could ever imagine or guess or request in your wildest dreams! He does it not by pushing us around but by working within us, his Spirit deeply and gently within us. In YOUR wildest dreams!*

Can you believe the endless possibilities and the infinite vastness of this promise? I believe this promise is no exaggeration! Listen, Hollywood has created some pretty wild movies, we have all been blown away by! But each one fails in comparison! When compared to the imagination and ability God has at His disposal to deliver His promises to His children, when they are willing to receive and step into the calling, they have been given.

Realize this, **if God put something down in your heart, a desire He gave you, at the very moment of conception, He started working behind the scenes to make your dream a reality** and has never quit working to bring it about. Right now, I encourage you to accept by Faith that you have been called to participate in, and believe God is constantly directing the right opportunities, to open up to and for you. I want to encourage you, to earnestly hang onto this word, and to this promise, until you reach the delivered promised land God has waiting for you.

What can you accomplish for the kingdom of God? What you can do, is not the question! What can't you do, with God involved in the equation, when you are willing to receive and pursue what you have been called to do? Right now, **I encourage you to believe that Jesus is supernaturally, arranging things in your favor!** Good things, great things, *amazing and fantastic things*, are being *prepared* and awaiting your arrival.

You may not see any of these things in the natural. And if seeing to believe has been holding you back, *then stop looking with your natural eyes and start focusing with your spiritual eyes of faith!* Trust and know that no matter what God has called you to do, God is, and has always been, guiding you, each and every step. **Know that it's not a matter of *if* God's blessings will come pouring into your life, but only *when* they will. *Because they will!***

Until then, keep asking. Keep standing. Keep believing. Keep hoping. And keep the faith! Ask God for a new and increased boldness, to step into your true calling. Keep thanking GOD. Keep declaring His Word. Meditate day and night, on His goodness that Jesus wants to give to you, knowing God is a rewarder of those who diligently seek Him. And above all else, **keep running with everything you have. *Run towards the light!***

CHAPTER 8

WHAT DOES A MOVE OF GOD LOOK LIKE?

Now that we're in a mindset to hopefully and continually pursue the calling God has placed on and over our lives, **what should we expect to see, when God reveals our calling and purpose?** What will be our role in the coming days of revival and the moving of God, which so many have prayed for? The Bible is full of amazing examples of God's power, still baffling minds some 2000 years later! So I must ask you, are you looking for more of the same, like we have seen thus far?

Or are you, full of anticipation and expecting to see something so impossibly different and supernaturally charged, there will be no way to deny it's from God? **When you do see it, will you be ready to share what you know about your relationship with Jesus?** Will you help reap the much expected and unbelievable harvest in the days to come?

> There is a story about a painting in a famous art gallery in France. The painting depicts two chess players, one of whom is Satan, who appears arrogantly confident, and the other is a man who looks forlorn. If Satan wins, he wins the man's soul. (The painting is now popularly known as "Checkmate" and was painted by Friedrich Moritz August Retzsch.)
>
> According to legend, a chess grandmaster came upon this intriguing painting in the Louvre, alongside other famous art, such as the Mona Lisa. The grandmaster stared a long time at the chessboard in the painting, and finally noticed something surprising. The typical interpretation of the painting—that the devil had the man in checkmate—was incorrect. Though the devil seemed to be the obvious victor, he was, in fact, not winning!

The chess player said to the tour guide, "You know, I'm a world-famous chess player. You're either going to have to change the painting or change the name of it, because this man still has one more move. The king still has one move left. He has not been beaten by the devil. He has one more move, and then the devil will be in checkmate."

What does a move of God look like? Sometimes it's visible, sometimes it's not visible, until it's time to be revealed! We live in a day and age, in which practically every Christian has said one time, or another, what this world needs is a move of God! 2 Chronicles 7:14 then usually gets quoted as what the church body considers to be the definition of a move of God, which says:

If My people who are called by My name will humble themselves, and pray and seek My face, and turn from their wicked ways, then I will hear from heaven, and will forgive their sin and heal their land.

By this definition, a move of God sounds to me like a salvation call, a come-to-Jesus moment. How about you? So, therefore, the first move of God someone witnesses in their life, I believe, is the moment of salvation and repentance from their sins, when they acknowledge Jesus is the Savior of the world! Asking Jesus to be the Savior of their world!

When and if you have the amazing privilege of witnessing the Power of God firsthand, **do you think the event will be like something you have witnessed before?** I can tell you from the amazing experience and the lasting impact of accepting Jesus as my personal Saviour some 50 years later, I'm going to say, "No!" Because, like every other encounter I've had with the Holy Spirit, I still search for the adequate adjectives to describe the experience!

I feel that the moving of God—and our experience of it—will be like something we never would think or dream. **It will be something so magnificent, we would never dream such an event is even possible.** Something so amazing, we probably will have trouble finding the words to describe what happened.

I can remember the first time I was slain in the Holy Spirit. It was to say the least, extraordinarily amazing. More than 34 years later, I still struggle to find adjectives great enough to describe how incredible the experience was, and still is for me! *Amazing magnificent, miraculous, stupendous, over-the-top,* even *euphoric,* all fail to tell you what I felt, and what I still remember from the experience. I recall those in attendance that day, when the power of God fell several yards away from me, **the same reverberations of the Holy Spirit and power that hit me, nearly knocked them off of their chairs as well.** The Holy Spirit's presence was so seemingly delicate, yet incredibly intense throughout the entire encounter.

How do you describe the experience of something so powerful it can shake the entire world, yet, so amazingly concerned with our well being, constantly keeping track of tears, while simultaneously calculating the number of hairs on our heads? So caring and attentive to us with gentleness and love—a love like we have never known and will never forget for all of eternity!

Does a move of God always have to be understandable to those who are witnessing or receiving, to be authenticated as a move of God? By my personal experience and review of the last paragraph, I can confidently say, "No."

A move of God, even when you don't understand it—when it doesn't feel exactly right and might be indescribable, is still a move of God. Jesus addressed this with the Pharisee's in chapter 12 of Luke. "A house divided against itself cannot, and will not be able to stand." So, when God moves, even when it feels completely foreign to your understanding, yet the experience will always produce amazing results. It's unfortunate, but not everyone can go, or is willing to go, to the level where God is calling them, and call the whole church to go.

We must be resilient and we must be steadfast! Because the more God calls us to go to the new levels of relationship He has designed for us, the more the accuser fights all the harder. To make what God is doing seem foreign, and to keep us from what God has prepared for us, and wants us to help others achieve and experience! Our part in all of this is to be a willing recipient. **And to be a willing recipient, we need to** strive to constantly be in the position to believe, accept and receive what God wants to pour into our lives, and through us to the world.

We must be willing to receive what God has for each of us. We must be willing to set aside all of our inhibitions and purely focus our desire to pursue and receive exactly what God has for us.

We must remember, wherever we are, no matter who is nearby, *we are always* and only in the audience of One, as far as our relationship with God is concerned. We should never question His direction and/or His plans for our lives!

> 2 Samuel 6:14-22 NIV — *Wearing a linen ephod, David was dancing before the Lord with all his might,* 15 *while he and all Israel were bringing up the ark of the Lord with shouts and the sound of trumpets.*

When was the last time you danced or praised the Lord with all your might? **Have you ever had crazy and passionate worship like David did, with and towards God?** I know in each one of our lives, there have been times we have exerted all of our passion and our being, one way or another at an event. Really? Ever been to a ball game? How about a concert, or a rally? Have there been times in your life you have pursued your relationship with the Lord at the same intensity level, before the Lord and to the Lord? **If not, why not?** If you have then, when was the last time that you did? And lastly, why isn't that your normal mode of worship? Let me see… "Never, nope, yes, yes, yes—sad to say but no, have not, sorry to say, don't ever recall doing that and never occurred to me to think of that as a normal form of worship!" Are those some of your answers? You know it's not too late to change any or all of your answers, and truly change your life in the process.

I believe a person can never be too much, or too over the top, when praise and worship to God is concerned. When we get carried away with our worship before God, our intensity level and method of worshiping is no one else's business! The moment of pure, uninhibited praise and devotion often inspires others, serving as a reminder that worship is personal and profound. Worship is the beginning of humility before the Lord. As though nothing else matters in the whole wide world, but the one most important thing of all.

How are you getting your worship on! I asked you that question because When we get carried away and lost in our worship, as David did, that's when we enter into the position to receive from God, in ways we can't even think, fathom, or imagine!

[If you don't know, or haven't studied David's life, I suggest you read the whole back story of why David worshiped the way he did on this one day.]

> 2 Samuel 6:16-22 NIV *As the ark of the Lord was entering the City of David, Michal daughter of Saul watched from a window. And when she saw King David leaping and dancing before the Lord, she despised him in her heart.* 20 *When David returned home to bless his household, Michal, daughter of Saul came out to meet him and said, "How the king of Israel has distinguished himself today, going around half-naked in full view of the slave girls of his servants as any vulgar fellow would!"* 21 *David said to Michal, "It was before the Lord, who chose me rather than your father or anyone from his house when he appointed me ruler over the Lord's people Israel—I will celebrate before the Lord.* 22 *I will become even more undignified than this, and I will be humiliated in my own eyes. But by these slave girls you spoke of, I will be held in honor.*

News flash! Not everyone is going to approve of your relationship with God, or the way you worship Him. And you shouldn't care about what anyone else thinks! As we read, and as David himself strongly notes, **it doesn't matter what everyone else thinks. The only thing that matters is what God thinks!** When we come boldly, confidently and expectantly into the presence of God, when we get in the frame of mind, the only thing that matters is what God thinks. I believe we will see God's will for our lives take shape in ways we can't even imagine or think would be capable of happening!

I heard Lindy Cofer of *Circuit Riders* at a worship conference one time. She sang the song, *Jesus the Healer*. **The song and her method of worship moved me to an amazing "Holy Ghost" encounter with God!** I suggest you listen to the song several times through, getting alone with God and being blessed.

Telling her Lindy is a passionate, visual worshiper! And as she went through her worship time, she had a time of testimony. She told of a period in her life when **certain people told her that her method, or style of worship, was too exaggerated,** distracting, and had too much energy on display. I remember her sharing, "I dialed back everything! I stopped moving so much and doing everything I had been doing." And then she noticed the presence of the Holy Spirit was nowhere to be found and the atmosphere of her worship had completely changed.

She said it was like, "I was in a spiritual funk and our worship sessions were completely flat." She then said something I have never forgotten. She questioned God and said, **"God, where are you and why aren't you showing up?"** And God's reply to her was, *"Because, Lindy, you are not showing up!"*

Our method, *how* we worship God matters! The Bible says God inhabits our praise and worship! The Hebrew word most used to mean inhabit is *"yashab,"* which means, to stay, remain, or dwell—as in to make one's home. By that definition, I would say God partakes in our worship sessions and the more we show up for worship sessions, I believe God does too. Isn't it exciting to think that God comes right into our space as we worship Him?

Still, some will say, "Come on, Charlie… I just don't worship that way. That's just not who I am!" Okay, you may feel that way—and I'm not trying to be antagonistic—but how is your method of worship working out for you? Is God's presence and the Holy Spirit showing up in a way that is blowing you away, or a gentle whisper?

I am convinced we need to be more like Psalm 150 when we are worshiping before the Lord. Psalm 150 declares repeatedly, "Let Everything That Has Breath **praise the lord!**" I've said it before and I'll say it again:

> When a person says they want to see a move of God and revival, they need to draw a circle around themselves. When they can't contain their praise and worship happening inside

their circle, they will witness a move of God! I'll take that one step further. When that move of God happens, no matter how they worship God in public, they won't be able to contain what happens inside their circle!

When God starts to move inside your circle, it doesn't matter what kind of person you are, how prim and proper you are, or how dignified you may try to be! What happens to you will be so explosive because **the energy of the Holy Spirit will be completely uncontainable!**

Dustin Smith of *Here Be Lions* helped write the song *Got to Let it Out*, and his powerful lyrics describe exactly what we're talking about!

> *I've got a praise that will break off heavy chains. I've got a song that makes hell begin to shake. I've got a shout that brings dead men from their graves. I've gotta let it out, I've gotta let it out...*
>
> *It's like a fire that's shut up in my bones. It's like a passion that's burning in my soul. It's running wild and I'm losing all control. I've gotta let it out, I've gotta let it out, I've gotta let it out!*
>
> *I'm gonna sing till I have no voice. Even then I'm gonna make some noise.*
>
> *I don't care what people say, I'm gonna praise You anyway.*

[If you haven't heard Dustin's song, I encourage you to search for his music, and the ministry of *Here Be Lions*. You will be blessed!]

Imagine millions of believers, locked arm in arm and singing a song like *Got to Let it Out*, in unison! —Oblivious to everything but lifting up the name of Jesus. —On the march, with this one thing as their main objective: **to take as many souls as possible with them to heaven. I believe this is what the move of God, the move coming on the horizon, is going to look like.** Why would we want, or be willing to settle for anything less than giving God our absolute best?

What we've been taught before, what we have experienced before, what we've been told to think and how to act before, needs to be reevaluated. Someone once told me when you're searching out something from God, don't take someone else's word for it, search it out for yourself. I would give you the same advice. **Don't take my word for it. Search it out for yourself. In the process you will find God and His amazing will for your life!**

We need to do as the Bible instructs us, "obtain a fresh anointing, a new wineskin mentality!"

> Mark 2:22 NIV — *And no one pours new wine into old wine skins. Otherwise, the wine will burst the skins, and both the wine and the wineskins will be ruined. No, they pour new wine into new wineskins.*

Because what God is getting ready to do, will burst our limited capacity to receive it if we don't! In our lives, in our church, with our families and in the world around us! God is looking for somebody to stand in the gap, to be counted faithful and courageous enough to say "**God, please help me receive what you have for me and empower me to do what you have called me to do.**" Are you that somebody? *Are you?* If not, will you be honest enough with yourself, to admit you need to ask God to help you become that somebody?

Ask to be ready to be God's hands, ready to be his feet, and to be the Voice of God in this day and age, proclaiming the message of Grace, until the whole world knows the Gospel Story. This story—the story of the world, the supernatural, amazing story of God and His son, Jesus—includes us all!

If you're going to be a part of God's army, **don't you think it's time you got off the sidelines and started putting some points on the scoreboard of eternity?** If you don't stand up and proclaim what you know, how many more of your friends and family will you stand by and see spend eternity in hell because you refused to get involved? Wow! That hits home—the difference one more willing laborer can make in the harvest of souls for the kingdom of Heaven!

As sobering as all this is, I must remind you that **you alone are responsible for your part of reaching the world with the gospel for Jesus!** "Who—me?" Someone else is not going to come along to replace and relieve you from what you are expected to do! ***You are the replacement! It's time you replicated yourself by winning someone else to Jesus!***

By all definitions, friend, we are in the last days— the end of time, as we know it! Truthfully, I believe (in our concept of time), it's been sudden death overtime, for quite some time! But I want you to know, it's not too late! God said, "He would not that none would perish!" And He doesn't want anyone to perish! But the fact remains, **people will perish, if we don't all do our part!** There's still time remaining to make our greatest impact yet for the Kingdom of God! Life changing impacts, which will be felt by so many for all of eternity!

Before I close this chapter, I'm going to do what us mid-westerners refer to as, "a country goodbye." Which in essence, is one more story, which will lead to another bit of dialogue.

I'm reminded of a childhood game we used to play called, *Red Rover*. In the game, two selected captains would pick teams from all the children, one-by-one, dividing the whole group into two teams. Each team would make a chain by linking arms with each other in one line, which faced the opposing team's line of linked arms. A team captain would then call out one person by name from the opposing line, saying "Red rover, red rover, send Charlie on over!" Then I would run directly into the opposing team's line, attempting to break through the linked arms of the human chain.

I remember running through the opposing team's line many times successfully. Each time I accomplished that task, I got to choose one of their team members at the broken part of the chain to become part of my team. But if I failed to break through, I became part of the other team's chain.

As exciting as that action was, I'm reminded of the even more exciting time in the game: being chosen to be a part of the team! There was great anticipation in the picking process, always hoping you weren't the last one. But then once you were on a team, it didn't matter how small or weak you were, as long as you were chosen, then you were a part of the team.

I go through all this to tell you, there is a spiritual element we can glean from this childhood game. In your relationship with Jesus, when you were chosen, or when you finally decided to be part of the coming harvest of souls for salvation, is irrelevant. The amazing fact is you have been chosen! And the fact you are reading these words right now, even pondering how much of an impact you can make for the kingdom of God, is the important thing. There are no coincidences in the kingdom of God—only God inspired and divine moments of opportunity.

Again, I ask you, "What will you do with this moment?" Friend, I want you to know, there's a point in everyone's life, when sitting on the fence of indecision seems like a defensible position. I know, because I sat there for a long time. Like me, and my time on the fence, your time defending your reasoning and positioning has come and gone.

I encourage you and suggest, **it's time to make the all-in decision of getting into a committed relationship with Jesus. Commit to what he's doing, and start playing to win**. Play like you have never played before! There is no other option for those of us who call ourselves Christians, but to help Jesus take as many souls with us—and away from the devil's grasp—as we can!

Are you ready? I trust by your decision I'll see you everywhere God leads you, working towards God's MVP trophy with the words, "Well done, good and faithful servant!" Billy Graham is reported to have shared that it takes 28 engagements or interactions of the gospel to reach someone for Christ. The first person thinks they did nothing, and the last person thinks they did all the work, when they lead someone to Jesus.

The truth is, **everyone** will receive a reward for their part in the harvest. I've been the first person to sow seed, and I've been given the privilege of being number twenty-eight to reap the harvest, and also the privilege of being every other number in between. *What will be your part, as we lock arms and* **Run Towards the Light?**

It really doesn't matter, because, I believe all of Heaven is aware and rejoices at every stage of a soul's redemption process—to **God be all the glory!**

What an **awesome opportunity** for us, to be a part of "Plan A" at all! And I say, "let's get busy!" Now—what say you?

CHAPTER 9

WHEN WILL ENOUGH BE ENOUGH?

D. Martyn Lloyd-Jones said, "Men and women no longer... exercise in sport as they used to. Instead, people tend to sit in crowds and just watch other people play.... And I fear that the tendency is even [presenting] itself in the Church."

As I thought about how the Lord would have me begin this chapter, I was reflecting on a conversation from earlier in the week. In this conversation with a friend of mine one of us brought up the improbable and heinous things we've witnessed over the last couple of years, and many which we've been told are the new norm.

We agreed—possibly, you will too—that what we are witnessing now is almost unbelievable. Some men now think they're women, and women think they're now men. Children can be cats or dogs nowadays, or anything they want to identify with. In fact, public teachers and the curriculum encourage such behavior!

And by the standard of the world, we're expected to smile, nod, accept everything at face value.

But it's not okay! Its not okay!! Not today, not tomorrow. Not any day of the week, or year! Thankfully, starting in January 2025, we are witnessing the explosive spiritual atmosphere of God's much anticipated correction and change, or mandate, in every part of the world.

It's no coincidence we are seeing the winner of the election, God's man of the hour, moving at warp speed. It's no coincidence either, that we are seeing the exposure of corruption in a victory of the 2020 cycle of politics, we would have never witnessed, if God would not have answered our prayers for revival!

Yes, the distractions by the accuser which everyone still faces daily, are so many we can't count them. Any given day, we are distracted again by the distractions we witnessed from the previous day's attempt at distracting us. The cycle repeats, designed with one focus in mind: to take our mind off of the devil's one track plan of "steal, kill, and destroy." It's his objective and focus that has never changed, to take as many souls as he can with him to hell!

Unbelievably, everything is happening in plain sight, in real time, right before our eyes. Meanwhile, innocent children, young girls and boys, are still being exploited, kidnapped, and sold into sex trafficking. People are still searching, trying to fill an empty hole—the void in their lives—with everything except the only One—Jesus—who will satisfy their hunger and desires.

Man-made killers, methamphetamine, fentanyl (drug-of-the-day), and the pharmaceutical drug manufacturing epidemic, and intervening surgeries (with many still unknown ramifications) are continually ruining lives. And each year the deaths increase at a record pace over the numbers of lives taken in previous years.

You would think, with everything going on in the world, there would be a stampede of people, stepping over one another, running in droves towards the light of God and the church. But, they're not! **Both the de-churched and the un-churched have stopped attending churches altogether** in massive numbers. Our nation has record high levels of zero attendance in the church! Sad to admit, but it appears that none of them are making an effort to come back.

Yet! And I say "yet," because I still believe we will see a turnaround for Jesus in the days ahead. The old battle cry for unity is, "United we stand, divided we fall." I keep wondering when the church and God's people are going to stand together and say, **"Enough! No more, Satan. We're not going to take anymore crap from you. We've had enough!"**

I wonder, where is the outrage. Where is the anger? Not towards God, but towards the accuser, towards the lowlife piece-of-work that the cunning accuser really is! **It's time we all went up to the so-called high places, took back what is ours,** tore the devil's kingdom down and burnt it to the ground, once and for all! Why do we put up with all of the noise? When we were made for so much more? And we've been given so many more tools than the ones we use daily to defend ourselves.

We act like we acknowledge all the sickening protests and events happening on the nightly news, and then act like, **"Oh well, there's nothing we can do about it, except pray."** *We don't even realize the true potential and power of such a statement!*

It's almost like we're oblivious to the never ending power we've been given to unlock the unlimited resources in Heaven—our spiritual WMD, or "Weapon of Mass Destruction" prayers.

Oh, victory in Jesus, my Savior forever!
He sought me, and He bought me with His redeeming blood.

Do you know that song? Do you believe those words describe your relationship with Jesus? Too many people know the words to that song, yet are far from understanding the power of them. They don't have any idea how to receive the *Victorious Life* God has already prepared for them, and walk in it. **Where is the visible fruit of Jesus' Victory in our lives?** I believe we've all been guilty, *(ouch!)* myself included, of having less than noticeable, far from abundant, spiritual fruit. Therefore, we're going to have to step up all our efforts, roll up our sleeves, and get to work.

As I have said, there is a new shift in the atmosphere; The optimism of victory in the air! **The Holy Spirit is getting ready to deliver an unbelievable new and fresh anointing!** It will be something like we have never seen. I believe it's time for the church to fully **embrace what God is getting ready to do.** It's time to take a step of unity, standing together to put action behind our words, so our testimony is noticed and actually means something.

Actions always speak louder than words, and truthfully, a Christian should never have to be asked to give their testimony. **Our testimony should be identifiable for everyone to see, by the way we live!** And if our testimony is not visible, maybe it's time to repent and reboot, like David throughout his life, continually did. There's no shame in repentance!

There is victory and redemption to be found in Repentance! It is long past the time of assessing what's going on. **We need to step up and**

get out of the boat of spiritual mediocrity. Jesus directly addressed his disciples' lack of faith. I believe the church's lack of faith needs to be addressed today. As I'm sharing this, I feel as though the Lord is giving us all a spiritual, Holy Ghost, call to action. This is a genuine, *whoever has ears to listen, better get to listening* kind of moment!

Can you hear the echo of Jesus' call to arms? We need to be like the prophet Ezekiel who said: *"Breathe...* **Oh Valley of dry bones.** *Get up off of your feet, and go to work!"*

In American football language: We are now at fourth-and-goal. The ball is on the line. God is saying, **"I'm looking for someone who will step up and out of the comfort zone, someone who will be a significant player on the field with My Son Jesus**, and run the ball of salvation into the end zone while the whole world watches the light of Jesus shine on all of humanity!"

I can remember in high school football, playing backup quarterback. Most times, I longed to be put into the game so I could show what I thought—or what I dreamed—I could do. But, there was this one night when our opponents were fierce competitors. Our quarterback was getting sacked right and left. Poor Mike, he was taking a beating. And I begin to wonder what would happen if he got hurt.

Instead of singing my favorite tune, "put me in coach," I was hoping and praying, "Oh, God, don't let him get hurt!" I didn't want to go in there and face the fierce giants, I mean, competitors! I remember thinking, "If they hurt the number one QB, what in the world would they do to number two?" Isn't it strange that simply the thought of fear can be immobilizing?

I love the story of Peter walking on the water! But when you think about that story, you must remember there were several guys in that boat, who let fear immobilize their faith. They did not bother to speak up, nor even try to get up and say, "Let me come too, Jesus!"

Now, If you feel like "walking on the water" is too much of an illustration to drive this point home, I can tell you something which might make you feel better! **Peter never thought he could walk on the water either,**

until he was called by Jesus to try. The rest is recorded Bible history. We still marvel and dream about that story.

Most Christians know what they ought to be doing, but they're not using their talents, or their God-given seed of faith, to any measurable amount of their ability. They haven't been faithful to their calling for years and even more years.

And far too many Christians have never even asked God what their calling is. I asked earlier about your calling, reader. **If you haven't asked God about your calling yet, what are you waiting for?** Seriously, I ask you, "What exactly are you waiting for?"

Don't even let one more person slip into eternity, without knowing Jesus, because of your neglect to ask, pursue, receive and step into your calling.

It's a sad fact, but far too many Christians have twisted the gospel over and over to fit their narrative and lifestyle. Remember what I said earlier, about making and breaking agreements that will keep someone from their calling? If a stranger to Christ witnessed their lifestyle, that unbeliever wouldn't be able to tell for certain if they were a Christian.

If Jesus Himself were to throw the ball to them in a football game, they wouldn't even be able to find the strength or the courage to run. And if they did run, they would probably run towards the opposing team's end zone! Because of the innocent, yet dangerous little agreements, even unknowing agreements, they had made with the strongholds in their lives! Thus, holding them back, from a fully committed and surrendered relationship with Jesus.

Friend—I hope by now that you can realize, I am speaking personally to you as a friend—It's time to wake up! Shots have been fired by the accuser, and continue to bombard us all. **People are dying without Jesus today, and they are going to hell in record numbers!** Does that bother you like it does me? The Bible says do not be weary of doing well. Do not think the efforts of your calling are ever made in vain. Every action, every conversation, every opportunity for the harvest, and every life that comes to Jesus, matters! You matter.

1 Peter 5:8 NKJV — Be sober, be vigilant; because your adversary, the devil, walks about like a roaring lion, seeking *whom* he may devour.

Would you agree that the Lord, by that statement of '*whom*', meant to warn everyone? Far too many people have read this scripture, but not believed that word pertained to them.

The devil has them convinced that the *handwriting on the wall* does not pertain to them! They're not in church. They are not walking in relationship with Jesus. They're not serving God at all! AND their lives and lifestyles are ***miserable*** at best…

People pretend everything is great, while projecting a false Facebook "godly and moral" lifestyle, while the truth is, their lives are falling apart. They may have a prodigal son or daughter, their marriage may be in trouble, they may be suffering from addictions, drugs, or drinking too much. The list goes on.

I know what it's like, my friend. I can relate. I was that person at one time in my life. By all accounts, everyone thought, or at least I believed everyone else thought that I was okay, while on the inside I was dying. You see, I thought as long as I had my father convinced nothing was wrong, I felt as though no one else's opinion mattered. But the truth is, the only opinion that matters is God's opinion. After my dad passed away, and I spent years running from my calling and trying to run from God, there was a finally a day of reckoning. I remember the night like yesterday, when the hammer finally dropped.

As I lay helplessly, convulsing on my kitchen floor, having one violent reaction after another, from too much of what I thought was helping me through the struggles of life, I remember thinking that I was always a good person. But as I lay there still flailing helplessly, I was forced to consider my life; **How had things gotten so messed up?**

I thought I could handle everything, but this time was different. This time I knew I was in deep trouble. Is this the way things would end for me? I was at a crossroad of *surrender* and *out-of-control*, but somehow I convinced myself that I was still in control of my own life.

Wave after wave of violent pain, reaction, and struggle came and went, for what seemed like an eternity. **During the worst moments, I would cross my fingers, lie through my teeth, and promise God** that I would stop what I'd been doing and serve Him. But in the calm between violent reactions, I would slip back under the control of my familiar strongholds where I had already made far too many agreements.

I believe though, as a final wave of torment came flooding over me, **there was one last chance given by a faithful God, and because of my mother's prayers.** The pain and anguish of trying to vomit something that wasn't physically there—not just the demon of addiction, but also the demonic stronghold of agreement—was miserably unbearable!

In that moment, I realized I could no longer bear all the burdens I had been carrying by myself any longer. And in that moment I said, *"Lord, if you help me and rescue me, I promise I will serve you the rest of my life!" But this time I meant it.* In that moment, God did exactly what I asked Him to do. God opened the floodgates of Jesus' Love, Grace and Forgiveness. He simultaneously rescued me from the clutches of the accuser, and I have never looked back.

It was like someone shut off a water faucet. Immediately, it was over. I wasn't a recovering addict, getting ready to celebrate sobriety, *I had been miraculously delivered! And I'm still praising God!*

Even as I write this, I think back on my moment of deliverance, and how it happened that night. I want to tell everyone, I was truly saved. I now realize all the excruciating torment and pain was caused by the demon of addiction, a powerful stronghold not wanting to leave, unwilling to be eradicated. And in the self-imposed, extended time of my struggle, and the moments of familiar agreement, the accuser would get one more last grip on me.

I believe the closer I came to deliverance, the more pain I felt each time the demon of addiction kicked, clawed, and screamed fighting against the Power of the Holy Spirit.

When I finally hit rock bottom, and I couldn't stand the pain any longer, I asked for God's help.

Just like the story of the prodigal, God came immediately running to my defense, and rescued me from the pain and mess I had made of my life! I tell you all this, because I want you to know God can help you to do what seems so utterly impossible to accomplish on your own! God did it for me! God's not a respecter of persons and I know God will do the same for you as well!!! No matter how far you may have gone, no matter how far you may think you are from God, even if you think you're at the end of your rope, God always has more rope. He can always reach you.

Jesus can, and He will, bring you back to restore your relationship with Him. *All you have to do is surrender and ask for His help! If that's you, won't you please surrender right now?*

You may say, "Charlie, that was a great story and all. And I'm happy for you. But I'm not suffering from addiction." Maybe you're not, but I can tell you from experience, my friend, that every—even the smallest—agreement with a strongholds, can and will grow into issues that can wreck you and eventually ruin your life, no matter who you are.

AGAIN, I pray if that's you, my friend, ask God to help **break all strongholds** off of your life. *Everything you have within your grasp and ability, either knowing or unknowingly, may be fueling the existence of those strongholds!*

Who am I to suggest such a thing? Someone who has been through the process and realizes the day to day struggle, of the battle. I am someone who is eternally thankful that God took the time—He made the investment—to show me how to be an **overcomer!** I'm just the proud messenger. But if you want to shoot something down, let it be me, and not the possibility of the redemption of your life.

HOW many more times will we, who think we have things all together, continue to lie to ourselves and everyone else? Continually saying, not only is this world going to hell in a hand-basket, but the house on the street we live in, is regrettably, right there in the hand-basket, and on the fast track to hell, or not very far from it. **How much more are we going to have to take, before we are willing to draw an undeniable line in the sand?**

How many more times will we have to get thrown under the condemnation bus, before we put some actions behind our words and finally take a stand to do something about what the devil has been doing to all of us, for far too long!

Isn't it time we wake up, smell the sweet aroma of the available spiritual coffee brewing, and realize we have the power to change our path? Yes, it is, Friend. And we can, if we're willing to step out of the boat of mediocrity, and embrace the change God wants to perform in us.

The church acts like they're really concerned with the moral decay of society. **But are they? Are we? Are you truly concerned?** It seems as though all of society is wrapped up, and concerned about themselves, and everything else, but the welfare of their own soul, their family's souls and the souls of humanity. I believe it's because society, in general, wants to stay in the shadows by remaining quiet.

They want to be perceived as naive and innocent when the world asks, "What would possess people to do these atrocities and commit violent crimes, freely and without regret, these days?" **That's like asking, "Why is the stove hot?" Don't you think? While knowing all along, there's a fire billowing uncontrollably inside the stove!**

Newsflash: It's not a fake news report of the political propaganda machine of the devil!

Since no one else wants to tell you, then I will tell you. Are you ready? It's a complete lack of Jesus in their heart, in their life, in their school, in their workplace, in their household. If you really want to know why, that is why. What possesses people to do the barbaric, heinous things they do!

Andre Crouch hit the nail on the head more than nearly 50 years ago when he wrote:

> *Jesus is the answer for the world today.*
> *Above Him there's no other, Jesus is the way.*
> *Yes, Jesus is the answer for the world today.*
> *Above him there's no other. Jesus is the way!*

Although he wrote those amazing and powerful words, Andre didn't come up with some newfound revelation. The answer has always been *Jesus*. It is, *Jesus*. And the answer will always be found in Jesus!

CHAPTER 10

PUT ME IN COACH

So, if the answer is *Jesus*, and the answer has always been *Jesus*. **Why are so many people wandering aimlessly through life without Jesus?** I think that's an important question. And it's what we're going to be covering next. And thus we have the title of this chapter. It reminds you what your involvement is going to mean from now on, and until Jesus calls us home.

> 2 Timothy 3:1-5 NKJV — *But know this, that in the last days perilous times will come: 2 For men will be lovers of themselves, lovers of money, boasters, proud, blasphemers, disobedient to parents, unthankful, unholy, 3 unloving, unforgiving, slanderers, without self-control, brutal, despisers of good, 4 traitors, headstrong, haughty, lovers of pleasure rather than lovers of God, 5 having a form of godliness but denying its power. And from such people turn away.*

Wow! What a totally amazing, and accurate description, of what we are now witnessing. It's the way things have become today. I'm going to ask you a question. One I already know the answer to, but I'm going to ask it anyway: **Can you relate to what I'm talking about?** Or are you oblivious to what's going on around you, in your world, your hometown, the house next door and on the street where you live?

Come on now people of God—Church! It's time for some honesty. We now see what 2 Timothy references, all day and night, on every news channel. There are very few who disagree. **But far too many people quietly turn off the light after the news. They do nothing with the day,** go to sleep, and then, *Bam!* it's *Groundhog Day*. Let's do this over and over and over again....

How many amber alerts do we have to get before we finally start paying attention to the alarm sounding repeatedly in the world around us?

I know this may feel like strong verbiage, but, the day for strong verbiage is ended—**It's time for action!** Believe what I say, one day soon, on judgment day, when we stand at the accountability table, this strong discussion will seem mild in comparison to what God passes before our memory in your own final episode of **This Was Your Life!**

At that point, there won't be any way to change what you have done with the time you were given. I'm telling you—and the Word of God tells you—there won't be one single person saying they wish they would've done less for the kingdom of God. Instead, millions—in fact, **billions will plead and beg for mercy, crying that they wish they had done more!**

And at that point, it will be too late.

We need to get the *I can* campaign going. Not the *I think I can,* campaign, But the *I Know I Can,* campaign. I'm talking about the "*I Can*" found in the Bible. "I can do..." how many things? Does your Bible read like my Bible? My Bible says:

> Phil.. 4:13-19 NKJV — *I can do all things through Christ who strengthens me.* **19.** *And my God shall supply all your need according to His riches in glory by Christ Jesus.*

These are the "I can" things I'm talking about!

* Taking a stand for Jesus!
* Visibly living your testimony and witnessing to someone by your actions, each day.
* Mentoring and lifting up someone who needs to be poured into, without expectation of return.
* Discipling everyone you can and replicating the gift you have been given.
* Extending grace much more than you think you can, more than is merited, or required.

* Listening to someone who is waiting to pour their heart out, asking God if He's real, and if He is ever going to send someone to show God's love in the flesh, to help them and care about them.
* Praying for the sick, believing for healing, locking your faith with theirs, expecting them to recover, and sticking it out until they receive their miracle!

"How should I prepare?" Here's some advice on preparing to serve God; **Stop worrying about preparation!** Leave the preparation to God and just get busy working for Jesus!

"What about the provision needed? What about money?" I'm sure there is far more money spent on coffee each day in the average believer's life, than is spent spreading the life changing message and story of the gospel.

Don't you think if God has called us to fulfill His vision of sharing the story of Jesus and His redemption, that God can and will supply the provision needed and required to do what He has asked us to do!

Friend, let me suggest something to you. **If "God will provide" is not how you think, then you need to get a new perspective of how extraordinarily big God is!** In case you didn't know this, God is far bigger than any box you may imagine putting Him in.

Proverbs 11:24-26 MSG — *The world of the generous gets larger and larger; the world of the stingy gets smaller and smaller. The one who blesses others is abundantly blessed; those who help others are helped. Curses on those who drive a hard bargain! Blessings on all who play fair and square!*

This is so much more than about spending our time and or our finances! **This is about an eternity, either with God, or an endless eternity of torment in *HELL!*** This is also about one day standing accountable for what we did for the kingdom of God at hand, here and now.

Again, let me say this loud and clear. No one is going to say they wished they had done less when they're standing at the accountability table of the Lord, on judgment day. Do you think God, in His infinite wisdom, would call us to do something for Him that He has not already, *in advance,* provided provisions and opportunities for us to use?

No matter how many opportunities—no matter how much help we may need, God has made everything available in abundance and at our disposal. Like the scripture declares, *We can do all things through Him.* Say it with me… "I can! I believe I can!"

Do you believe we can do all things?

Cleverly and cunningly, the devil, through one innocent act of agreement after another, has convinced many of God's children to think and act like *they* can't do anything! So, therefore *they don't even attempt to do anything!*

And, God forbid, if we do decide to attempt something, we listen to the accuser's line of reasoning when he warns, "You're going to have to do a whole lot more than you bargained for, if you get involved!"

Isn't this the whole point of getting involved in the first place—to actually make a difference, and to be involved in something bigger than your own efforts can accomplish? Let me remind us all of some facts. The whole time Jesus was here on this earth, did Jesus' disciples perform any miracles? Who, other than Jesus, was responsible for performing even one single miracle before the cross?

NO ONE. THAT'S WHO!

Did they feed the masses, with just a sack lunch?

Did they make the deaf hear?

Did they cause the lame to walk and the blind to see?

I'll remind us and ask again, did they perform any miracles?

Did they even cure the common cold?

I'll tell you what did happen. And it happened more than once… They were lectured on how little they were willing to use the more than adequate ***measure*** of faith they had been given.

Many times Jesus said, ***"Oh ye of little faith!"*** And yet we read in the book of John that Jesus promised them, and every believer who would come after them, we who would use our faith and believe, would be able to do all the things Jesus did and even greater things than Jesus did.

> John 14:12 NKJV — *Most assuredly, I say to you, he who believes in Me, the works that I do he will do also; and greater works than these he will do, because I go to My Father.*

When Jesus first spoke those words to them, I imagine they didn't quite know what to think! To tell you the truth, **most of us even today still don't know quite what to think about the power and authority given for all of us to use**, exactly what we've been given, and the reasons why we have been given such great power!

"I'm sorry, John," Peter probably asked (pure conjecture here), "Did Jesus just say what I thought He just said?" There's not even enough pen and paper in the world to record everything Jesus did in His earthly ministry. And by writing Jesus' powerful and prophetic words, John boldly declares what His believers will be able to accomplish because of His ascension to Heaven!

"And we…" *We?* It's talking about you and me, friend. *We* are going to do greater things than Jesus has done!

"Why yes, Peter," John wrote in response, **greater things** you and I are going to be able to do! **Even now** you may be thinking, was Jesus talking to the entire church? Yes, Jesus was talking about everyone who would come after Him!

Again, I tell you to grab hold of your spiritual seat belt! But more importantly, **grab hold of your God-given measure of faith** and this amazing promise: "**Yes, he was speaking to me,**" "Most surely I say to you, he who believes in Me, the works I do [Your Name here] will also do." And why would I tell you to do such a thing? Because Jesus said you could. So why wouldn't or shouldn't you do so? Jesus said, and this applies to every Christian, "If you believe in Me, child of God… greater things shall you do, because I go to my Father!"

I feel I must remind you of another promise. Jesus is with the Father, interceding for us, for everything we set out to do—those things Jesus has called us to do, and said through scripture, we can do. We must not forget this, but consistently remind the devil of this promise, and what it does in our fight against evil— **everything evil!**

The disciples were wondering, "How would this happen? Greater things than Jesus did, wow." I know it's hard to get your hands around this. People 2000 years later wonder the same thing. **Is this promise—this Word—still true for us?** I think we ask and question our own limited understanding too often, because truthfully, we know the answer.

Yes, this word and promise is, and will always be true, because God's word is true, and never changes. *There's not one promise God ever made that he didn't intend on keeping!*

Jesus always knew, the commission He called us to would only be possible once the Provision of The Holy Spirit was revealed. Then both they and we, would be able to possess God's Power in our lives. And man, oh man, was Jesus right! It was what I referred to earlier in chapter 4. Yes, that's right, "The infilling of the Power of The Holy Spirit" in Acts chapter 2. That's when God's amazing plans for all believers—not limited to just that time—began with the Holy Ghost promise of supernatural acceleration. **When the Holy Spirit arrived on the scene, everything became possible,** because of the power in our salvation relationship and the comfort and teaching of the Holy Spirit.

To this day, The Holy Spirit is helping and equipping God's children, through their salvation relationship with Jesus and infilling, to consistently accomplish the impossible. **The devil didn't have a clue that the Holy Spirit was coming. He had no battle plan to fight against Him! And praise the Lord, the devil still has no clue how to battle Him, or anyone, who is working through the power and infilling of the Holy Spirit.**

If you can't tell already, my friends, let me make it clear to you now—this really excites me! I'm excited about the relationship I have with the Holy Spirit, as you should be! I'm excited about what The Holy Spirit does, empowering me in my fight against the spiritual battles that every Christian fights.

How about you? Are you excited about your relationship with the Holy Spirit? If not, why not? God sent The Holy Spirit so you could have that exciting relationship. So, why aren't you excited?

Are you seeking and cultivating your relationship with the Holy Spirit? Every Christian should be!

All of Hell is shaking in their boots at me even mentioning this thought, the possibility of you becoming a *Spiritually Filled Christian*.

> Acts 2:16-18 NKJV — *But this is what was spoken by the prophet Joel: And it shall come to pass in the last days, says God, That I will pour out of My Spirit on all flesh; Your sons and your daughters shall prophesy, Your young men shall see visions, Your old men shall dream dreams. And on My menservants and on My maidservants I will pour out My Spirit in those days; And they shall prophesy.*

What happened on the day of Pentecost was, and is still, amazing. Those who were there freely received what scripture declares is still for us to receive today. What they did with the gift revolutionized the world with the Power of the Holy Spirit and the Gospel of Christ—the very same power and relationship with the Holy Spirit of God that is available today. There is no other way possible to do what Jesus said would be greater than what He did, except, by receiving the power of His Holy Spirit, sent to equip all of His Children. And it is through the in-filling of power, the Holy Spirit enables you.

Twenty-nine years ago, I came to the realization I could actually receive and accomplish what Jesus said I could, and what God was calling me to do! Was I nervous? Absolutely! Yes, I was nervous. Thankfully, I was more hungry in my relationship with Jesus, for what God said I could have, His heavenly gift of the Holy Spirit, than I was scared by the fear tactic of religion. Dead religion echoes the accuser, saying that the power of the Holy Spirit isn't of God, but of the devil!

But I know, without a doubt that, without having received the gift of the Holy Spirit, I never would be where I am today. I never would have accomplished a fraction of what God called me to do. So many things God called me to, I wasn't even qualified for. But, I didn't have to worry, because Jesus qualified me through the Power of the Holy Spirit of God living in me. **He supernaturally qualifies and empowers me daily with His ability.**

My prayer is that you would desire the same supernatural experience in the way God has created especially for you. The Holy Spirit will empower and qualify you in the same way.

Do you have to pursue and receive the gift of the Holy Spirit? No, it's not required for you to have a relationship with Jesus. **However, I want to remind you, one more time, that the Holy Spirit is a gift**. He is a gift from God the Father. Jesus lived, was crucified, died, and rose again. He conquered sin, Satan and hell forever, for you to have a gift from God, sent straight from Heaven after Jesus made His ascension to be with His Father!

You might be the exception to the rule—but I've never seen anyone *not* want to open all of their gifts, no matter what the occasion. Isn't it time we took back what was stolen from us, what has been rightfully ours all along? The answer is, "Yes, a trillion times yes, it's time!" It's time that all Christians took back what has always been rightfully ours. It's time we accept our gift and use it for the glory of God.

Let's take it back with a vengeance to accomplished everything for the kingdom that God has set before us!

Take back what's been ours all along, and live the abundant, amazing life we have been given!

Everyday we don't share the Gospel, everyday we don't lift up the name of Jesus, everyday we don't try to at least make a difference, somehow for the cause of Christ, *is another chance of victory for the accuser!* Our failure to act is another opportunity for Satan to steal, kill, and destroy another life and take them to hell.

The Holy Spirit is still willing to make a way and empower each and every one of us to do what we've been called to do. And we are all called to share the message of the Gospel, often in ways we can't even imagine. But, He is a gentleman. God won't push His miraculous ways on us. He waits for us to decide to ask and to receive His gift.

We are the deciders.

You decide!

What will you do today with what you know? **I Challenge you to pray and ask God to fill you with the Amazing Gift of the Holy Spirit!**

I challenge you to embrace a fully Holy Ghost mindset. Get into the fight you've been called to, like you never have before. Grab hold of the Holy Spirit. Grab hold of the Amazing Power God has given you. Start **spreading** the gospel message. **Run continually towards the light!** Run towards the prize of eternity. Make a *rest-of-your-life* commitment to take **the absolute most souls to heaven with you**, as possible! To take a stand with God's Army and scare the hell out of the devil!

The devil thinks he has the church, backed into a corner of despair, delusion and surrender, without the ability to maintain our bearing, or even to engage our moral compass anymore!

Did you know that the entire population of Israel, God's chosen people who made their way of liberation from slavery and Egypt's captivity—those people: None of them—*not one single one of them*—entered the promised land. And Here's why. They forgot who they were and *whose* they were. Only those born after the exodus from Egypt, entered the Promised Land. Everyone else died before it happened, even Moses.

History does not need to repeat itself. We, who will listen—we, who will get up off the couch—can make a difference. We, who will commit ourselves to God, can alter history the way the disciples did after receiving the power of God from the Holy Spirit. This is what we, the church, should be shouting from every rooftop, "When will enough ever be enough?"

When will God's children ever get tired of being manipulated by the devil and his shenanigans? When will we finally get mad enough at the devil, to fight back in unity together, with the power God so graciously gave us? Collectively we can clobber him good, with a gift that is more than sufficient to render him powerless. We can give him his marching orders, for good!

If we all agree and commit to work together for Jesus, there's nothing we can't do or accomplish. Will you ask God what your part will be in this final stretch of history—the final days of the church? This is a journey we're all on together, one Church and one plan for our spiritual destiny! I have made that commitment. That's why I wrote this book. That's why we are having this conversation.

Now if we're all in agreement, let's get busy for Jesus and get to work!

What do you say? I may not see you now, friend, but I can't wait to see you put up some big numbers on the scoreboard of eternity. And with me, there is a host who are cheering you on from Heaven!

CHAPTER 11

HURRY UP, HAVE FAITH AND WAIT

Have you ever heard the words, "Hurry up and wait"? Many military men and women have heard these instructions, state, federal, corporate employees. They sounds somewhat contradictory to me. How about you? If it were anything other than spirituality, it would be! As long as man is in charge, those words, "Hurry up and wait," at best represent incompetence, chaos and disappointment!

When those words are spoken in a spiritual context, and God is in charge of the details, there is a love, forgiveness, grace, mercy, favor and peace which passes all understanding, to be found in the act of our obedience and waiting as instructed.

Another word that could be substituted for waiting, is resting! Not to be confused with doing nothing, or inaction. **Resting is not *doing nothing*. Spiritual resting in your faith, isn't anything like that, at all!** Spiritual resting is the act of doing everything you can, by depending on your salvation relationship that you have with Jesus for everything and your God-given faith to believe!

Resting in God's ability doesn't rely on your self-effort to help.

How hard is *resting* to do? Not as easy as it seems, but not as hard as you think also. Is it doable? Why, yes it is! It's a matter of using one's faith to wait until the Lord recognizes even the slightest amount of faith, declares the timing is right, and **shows up to show off His capabilities**.

Am I making light of how faith works? No. And I don't mean to equate it to the military, the government, or anything else. There were many instances in the Bible, where such times and events like what I described, indeed happened. For instance, at the battle of Jericho,

When did the wall fall down? The wall fell down when the people in faith rose to the task at hand, waited on God's timing, being obedient for 7 days. Then God showed up and He showed off.

What about the story of Goliath? Goliath fell when **a small boy showed up with faith, waited on God's timing, stepped out in obedience, with 5 carefully selected stones and a piece of rawhide.** Then God showed up and He showed off. In pretty much every example and story we read in the Bible, when someone actually showed up with the amount of faith which the Bible says is a tiny amount required to move God's hand— when that person stepped out in obedience and waited—God showed up and showed off!

> Isaiah 40:31 NKJV — *But those who wait on the Lord Shall renew their strength; They shall mount up with wings like eagles, They shall run and not be weary, They shall walk and not faint. But teach me Lord, teach me Lord to wait.*

Can you see how Isaiah is coming from a point of need, and also, of amazing realization? He is sharing his learned moments of faith through resting, what is amazingly possible, by the defeat of his self effort. How, if a believer is willing to do the same, by bringing our needs to the Lord and laying them at his feet, the Lord, in His faithfulness, shall refresh, renew and replace our need with His abundance, of every good thing.

When we get to this place of tiredness, we normally feel like we have nothing left to give. Our self-effort says there's no sense in trying with our ability any longer. We feel like we have spent everything we have. We have normally exhausted all of our limited resources, and our own understanding.

Normally, when a person repeatedly does the same thing over and over without achieving the desired results, it's called *insanity*. Here's where we need to change our line of thinking. Here's what I mean by that—What would be possible in our lives if we started with an admission of exhausted efforts and attitude of exhausted abilities, from the first moment of our need? **Wouldn't the posture of faith, dependence and resting in God's promise and ability, be the most amazing place to start?** The undeniable answer is, *"YES!"*

This is why the position of our weakness makes more sense—in fact, the most sense possible. **It's a way to hurry up and get to the God, I need you part of faith**—to start with the humble willingness—to admit defeat of our own self-effort from the very beginning. Doing so is to invite God to be God in every situation that we need His help, in every area of life, even where we don't realize we need Him, and from the very start of our effort.

Steven Furtic said something that stuck with me recently. He said;

> *Confidence in God's promises, without commitment to His processes, is not dependence… It's delusion.*

When Steven Furtic mentioned this, I wrote it down to remember and think about it, specifically because of its relevance to this teaching.

Our human nature always wants the end result *before our complete surrender* and willingness of commitment, doesn't it? We will never achieve the results we're looking for, without having faith in the "waiting process of faith" God wants to take us through! Which is the route (Plan A) God's flawless plans ultimately deliver us to, and where we are thinking and wanting to go!

The sweetest reward is, realizing God's reveal is always so much better than our anticipated results, each and every time!!

> Mark 8:1-5 MSG — *At about this same time he again found himself with a hungry crowd on his hands. He called his disciples together and said, "This crowd is breaking my heart. They have stuck with me for three days, and now they have nothing to eat. If I send them home hungry, they'll faint along the way—some of them have come a long distance."* 5 *He asked, "How much bread do you have?"*

Jesus' expectation was enormous. Did He ask the disciples to feed everyone? What did Jesus ask for from them? What did they give Him? They gave Jesus what they had, when it wasn't even theirs, right? What did they give to Jesus? I suspect what they gave Jesus was probably a leftover. It wasn't a freshly prepared meal, but a leftover the boy's mother had sent for her son's lunch. Who said leftovers weren't delicious, or valuable in the hands of God?

> I once read the story of a family, who was sitting down at the dinner table for their evening meal. One of his girls wasn't happy because they were having leftovers, and she complained about it. The dad was not happy with the complaining, and he spent a few moments explaining why she needed to be more thankful for what she had.
>
> To make sure she understood his point, he decided to make her say the blessing for the food, and gave her instructions as to how her prayer should demonstrate her appreciation for what she had. When he finished instructing, she bowed her head, praying: "God, thank you for this food... again."
> — Heather Marshall, Reader's Digest, 5/03

So many times, we are reluctant to even give God what we have, because we don't think God can take what we have and make it work to provide what we need. That's worth reading again.

In those moments, we should be thankful for what we have. And we should be willing to share what we have, so God can supernaturally bless and turn what we already have, into what we truly need. It's not up to us to decide what God can do, or what God needs to do it. We don't control how He works to meet the needs of His Children. We simply offer what we have to His work. The most important thing is to expect in faith no matter what we possess, even if we don't have anything at all! God is willing to keep His promises to us and be faithful to us in each situation of need as it comes.

> I read another story of a minister's wife who was a wonder at conserving food. She rarely threw any food away. One meal she gave her husband nothing but leftovers. He was not enthusiastic about it. He began to pick at his food and only ate a little, but had not given thanks.
>
> His wife smiled sweetly, and gently said to him, "Dear, you forgot to say the blessing."
>
> He looked at her and responded, "Sweetheart, if you can't show me one item on the table that hasn't been blessed two times already, I can't see what another prayer can do for it."

Did you know that you can pray over and over, and still be dependent on your self-effort? ***Our faith only becomes active, when we pray with complete dependency, relying only on God's abilities, not our own.***

> Mark 8:16-21 MSG — *Meanwhile, the disciples were finding fault with each other because they had forgotten to bring bread. Jesus overheard and said, "Why are you fussing because you forgot bread? Don't you see the point of all this? Don't you get it at? Remember the five loaves I broke for the five thousand? How many baskets of leftovers did you pick up?" They said, "Twelve."* 20 *"And the seven loaves for the four thousand—how many bags full of leftovers did you get?" "Seven."* 21 *He said, "Do you still not get it?"*

Jesus was saying, loud and clear: *Wake up, boys and smell the coffee, it's not about what you think you have, it's about what I can do, when you put the most important thing you possess in My hands.* Jesus was telling them: *You already have everything you need. It's your faith and trust in me that I'm looking for.*

They had witnessed Jesus do the miraculous twice! Jesus had fed—by some estimates—as many as 35,000 individuals, with the contents and caloric value of two happy meals. Jesus, being the great teacher He is, took the opportunity as a teaching moment. One to be studied and discussed, pondered, written about, and praised for all of eternity!

Then, it seemed only ten minutes later, the disciples had already forgotten the miracle they witnessed, again! All of them worried: *A whole loaf of bread is not going to be enough to feed the few who are on the boat with Jesus!*

Let's be truthful, if we're willing to admit it, we are a lot like the disciples, and they are a lot like us. "Brothers from another mother? Human nature is human nature! We all have needs, the same way the disciples did, don't we? We pray and ask God to meet our needs, and He does. And then ten minutes later, another situation arises, and instead of having *carry over,* or *bridge gap* faith, from the last miracle God provided, we revert back to doubting Him.

We tend to forget our last victories, and not unlike the disciples, we revert back to square one, thinking, *how in the world are we going to solve this dilemma—We don't have enough food to feed these people?* Or in our case, we think we don't have enough resources to meet our own needs. *Bam!* It's *Spiritual Groundhog Day* once again!

So Jesus reacts in a way that no one will ever forget. Jesus says, "Stop, look and listen to what you do have, and then be willing to give it over and watch the impossible happen every time a need arises.

We can't do it, but Jesus can. We don't have the resources, but God does. If we're ever going to succeed in the ways we say we want to, we need to continuously replace "we," with "He!" Because, **He can, He does, He will, He wants to, He has the resources to do whatever we ask of Him, if we can only believe!**

What exactly is God's will for our lives? Many have asked! Many have a reluctance to accept God's will for their lives, because they're unaware how much God wants to do for them, and how much God truly wants to bless them. Not one day, eventually, *in the sweet by and by*, but in the immediacy of here and now. If that's you, then you can stop trying to put God in a box and limit what He wants to do for you.

> John 10:10 NKJV — *The thief does not come except to steal, and to kill, and to destroy. I have come that they may have life, and that they may have it more abundantly.*

We all have both mountain top, as well as valley experiences. What we fail to realize is that Jesus is right there for us in every situation, willing and able to meet and to exceed our every need. We only have to allow Him to use what we have.

Do you believe that statement? Then I suggest you do it. Let go of what you do have. Get ready for God to bless you, beyond your wildest expectations!

> Luke 21:1-4 NKJV — *And He looked up and saw the rich putting their gifts into the treasury, 2 and He saw also a certain poor widow putting in two mites. 3 So He said, "Truly I say to you that this poor widow has put in more than all; 4 for all these out of their abundance have put in*

> *offerings for God, but she out of her poverty put in all the livelihood that she had.*

What those two coins represented was everything the woman had left. Those coins really were her left overs—the ones she would need to survive. She obviously had no more, because the Bible says those were the *last two she had!* Two coins when you have a hundred coins, is no big deal. Two coins when you have two coins, and you are a widow with no source for more—that's a big deal! **Sometimes, we feel like what we have is not enough, even for God.**

But, like this widow woman, we need to realize whatever we do have is enough. In the hands of Jesus, it will always be enough. Never will it not be enough, but always ***more than enough*** for God to work and perform any miracle. If we are just willing to let go of it, and let God do what His Word declares that He will do. So, hurry up and place all your faith in Jesus' ability to deliver everything God has given Him. And God has given Him everything, to lavishly disperse whenever He sees our faith in action. So wait on Jesus to do what His Father has given Him the unlimited ability to do.

Let's look at the story of the prophet Elijah. It's a full illustration of "Hurry Up And Wait Faith!" And it's one of my favorite stories of Faith found in the Bible.

> 1st Kings 17:7-16 MSG — *Eventually the brook dried up because of the drought. Then God spoke to him: "Get up and go to Zarephath in Sidon and live there. I've instructed a woman who lives there, a widow, to feed you."* 10-11 *So he got up and went to Zarephath. As he came to the entrance of the village he met a woman, a widow, gathering firewood. He asked her, "Please, would you bring me a little water in a jug? I need a drink." As she went to get it, he called out, "And while you're at it, would you bring me something to eat?"* 12 *She said, "I swear, as surely as your God lives, I don't have so much as a biscuit. I have a handful of flour in a jar and a little oil in a bottle; you found me scratching together just enough firewood to make a last meal for my son and me. After we eat it, we'll die."*

Earlier when we read about the disciples, they weren't aware of what they had around them, right? This woman, however, was more than aware of what she had, and of what she did not have. And what she was telling him was, she did not have food to feed him, let alone feed herself or her son.

> **13-14** *Elijah said to her, "Don't worry about a thing. Go ahead and do what you've said. But first make a small biscuit for me and bring it back here. Then go ahead and make a meal from what's left for you and your son. This is the word of the God of Israel: 'The jar of flour will not run out and the bottle of oil will not become empty before God sends rain on the land and ends this drought.'"* **15-16** *And it turned out as he said—daily food for her and her family. The jar of meal didn't run out and the bottle of oil didn't become empty:*

God's promise was fulfilled to the letter, exactly as Elijah had delivered it. She took Elijah's prophetic word and ran with it. **She couldn't wait, she hurried to get through the *try me* part and on to the *wait and see* part!** I'm sure every morning without fail, she hurried with expectancy to the jar of flour and bottle of oil, happily rejoicing, there would be enough for each day. Again, and again, and again, she trusted and saw, day after day, after day, after day! And as a reward of her trust and undeniable faith, God did not let her diligence of faith go unrewarded. And God won't let your diligence of faith go unrewarded either.

God always makes possible what seems impossible, for those who are willing to give Him what they have, to trust Him and to wait upon Him to fulfill what He says He will do!

> I want to take a moment and share a story I heard a while back, about a man, waiting on a woman. It seems this man, Wilbur, was visiting a local department store with his wife. They had just purchased a piece of luggage and a cooler. As Wilbur browsed in the shoe section of the store, carrying his new purchases and waiting for his wife to finish the rest of her shopping, a sales saw him. The Male clerk greeted him kindly then asked if he could be of assistance. "No, thanks," Wilbur replied. "I'm just waiting for my wife."

At that point, another man who had been sitting in the department longer than Wilbur said, "I'm waiting for my wife, too, but I never thought to bring lunch and an overnight bag!"

Perhaps you can relate to this like me. One of the first things I was told before I got married was to get used to waiting on a woman. In fact, someone gave me a copy of Brad Paisley's song, *Waiting on a Woman*, with Andy Griffith in the video, telling this story.

I thought it was a cute and funny, but I also thought, truly, the only thing that makes you willing to wait on any one is the fact that you love them. We have been told over and over how much God loves us—so much that God gave His only begotten Son Jesus to die for us, so we could avoid hell's eternal damnation and spend forever with Him!

I believe the most significant way we show our love for God, is by using our faith to trust and wait. **Believe that Jesus will do exactly what His never failing word promises and declares He will do for us.** That, my friends, is our way of showing God our love and trust for Him. It's like what *Mercy Me* sings in the song, *Even If*;

> *They say it only takes a little faith to move a mountain.*
> *Well, good thing a little faith is all I have right now.*
> *But God, when You choose to leave mountains unmovable.*
> *Oh, give me the strength to be able to sing,*
> *"It is well with my soul"*
>
> [Chorus]
> I know You're able
> And I know You can
> Save through the fire
> With Your mighty hand
> But even if You don't
> My hope is You alone
> I know the sorrow
> And I know the hurt
> Would all go away
> If You'd just say the word
> But even if You don't
> My hope is You alone

Trusting and waiting on the Lord, and the willingness to do so, is a recurring theme in the Bible, with Great Results and great reward. The Bible doesn't say there won't be setbacks, or problems. But, there will be great results, if we don't quit the pursuit, and **Run Towards the Light of Jesus, to receive His promises!**

Abraham and Sarah waited on the Lord and they finally gave birth to a son. God's promise was fulfilled, and they became the father and the mother of many nations. With their descendants numbering more than the stars in the sky and the sands in the sea. Joseph was sold into slavery by his brothers. He eventually wound up in prison. But Joseph never lost heart and never stopped waiting on God, to bring about the dream God gave him as a young boy. **God honored his waiting and his faith. Joseph went from the prison to the palace—from a nobody, to a very important somebody.** God's faithfulness, honored faithfulness in Joseph. Faith promoted and allowed Joseph to become a Ruler over all of Egypt.

And by doing so, saved his own family and the entire nation of Israel, as well as all of Egypt, from starving in a widespread famine. Those are great stories. In fact, the Bible is loaded with fantastic stories about real life situations and real life people, prevailing over real life situations, just like us, our lives, and the challenges we face!

Miraculous, God-ordained, happy storybook endings, only brought to fruition, when they waited upon the Lord! In these events God was present and he allowed them to happen, to strengthen and to give tremendous hope, still today, to all who hear and read them.

The same could be said of you today. Yes, you friend! Don't shake your head, "no!" I challenge you to remember the many times God has helped you overcome life's situations. We all have Bible worthy testimonies, which should be shared whether we will share them, or not. Amazing moments where God stepped in and did something miraculous, for each and every one of us.

I don't know about you, but there are so many times in my life I have either thought or said, I don't know how it happened. But, when I finally got to the waiting and resting in my faith part of my circumstance, and got out of the way, God came through for me. What is possible in each one of our futures, if we are willing to hurry sooner to the waiting on God's part?

I encourage you, because it's more honest to think, "What's not possible?" in our own future, when we are willing to hurry to our *faith and wait* part of the equation. If we are willing to wait on God with our expectation of faith, that He has already given to us, there is nothing out of the realm of possibility, for each and every one of us!

What are you waiting on God for today? Do you feel a sense of urgency, or one of reluctance to let/make yourself trust God in the waiting? I encourage you to not only hurry up and get to the waiting part, but to start each time, in the beginning moment of your need, admitting the defeat of your self-effort. Simply and confidently start with faith, waiting and resting in the amazing ability God has given Jesus, to bless you!

Friends, I encourage you, *you can have complete confidence!*

God's timing is always perfect. The same way God came through for you the last time you were in need, you can depend on God to do it again, and again. Every time you hurry up and wait, believe He will!

CHAPTER 12

NOTHING ELSE MATTERS

I did not come up with this, but I sure do agree with the Someone who once said: "Destiny is not a matter of chance, it is a matter of choice; it is not a thing to be waited for, it is a thing to be achieved."

Wow! I have a choice in my Destiny? Yes. And if you're still reading, this is where I tell you that your pursuit and diligence to *Run Towards The Light* is what determines your destiny and your legacy.

What do you think your destiny and legacy will look like? What do you want your destiny and legacy to look like? What are you actively doing and what are you knowingly leaving behind, to let the world know you did something of significance?

How will you be remembered, as far as the kingdom of heaven is concerned? I believe the greatest answer that could be given for the last question is: *nothing else mattered to them*. And I believe in finding the greatest answer given, a person will also have revealed their destiny in the process!

What we do for the kingdom of heaven, is the most important thing we'll ever do in life. The Bible says our life is like a vapor, here one minute and gone the next. The Time In Between is the only thing of significance that is going to be remembered. The only accomplishment that will stand the test of time, of what we each of us actually did with our lives!

As we move on into this next chapter, we're going to be talking about David a little more. David had many triumphs for the kingdom of God. David also had several low moments in his walk with the Lord. In the end, what was it about David that garnered the words, "Well done thou good and faithful servant"? There are some who think it was all of David's triumphs. Truthfully, I believe there were many things praiseworthy as to the reason God said what He said to David.

Was it the way David worshiped? How about the way David fought victoriously in battle? Or maybe it was the way David praised God with his words that we read so often in the Psalms? Could it have been the way David repented when he made mistakes and sinned against God? A combination of all those things is why David is remembered as "a man after God's own heart."

Let's look at a time in David's life, when he was down. While he knew he was down, I don't believe there was ever a time when David believed he was *out*. Generally during those times of discouragement, that's when David praised God the MOST, in spite of the way things looked! **David—praising God no matter what moment he was in—found *renewed* strength, from a faithful, loving God.**

Let's look at the Psalms as an example. In Psalms 23, when David said, "The Lord is my shepherd, I shall not want," I believe this realization took David to the Victor's circle of his need every time. And the same realization will take each one of us to the Victor's circle, in our need! When you come to the realization that as long as God, through his amazing Son Jesus, is your Shepherd, then nothing else will matter—ever—no matter what!

> Psalms 56:1-4,8,10,11 MSG — *1-4 Take my side, God—I'm getting kicked around, stomped on every day. Not a day goes by but somebody beats me up; They make it their duty to beat me up.*
>
> *When I get really afraid I come to you in trust. I'm proud to praise God; fearless now, I trust in God. What can mere mortals do? 8 You've kept track of my every toss and turn through the sleepless nights, Each tear entered in your ledger, each ache written in your book. 10-11 I'm proud to praise God, proud to praise God. Fearless now, I trust in God; what can mere mortals do to me?*

When we read this, to put this in proper perspective, David is a prisoner in a foreign land. David has been on the run for years, fleeing for his life, every moment. He's trying to get away from King Saul, and what does he do? David runs away from his enemy, right into another enemy. David runs into the Philistine army and is captured.

I imagine right about now, (and I'm not sure if he would be saying this) I probably would be saying, "Hello Hey God! Hey, Great God of Israel, I didn't sign up for this! Hey God, remember when you said I would be the King! Hey God! You made it known, by the prophet Samuel, what your intentions were for me and all of Israel! Hey GOD, do you remember these conversations! Hey God, I haven't forgotten one single thing. But **I'm thinking, maybe,… just maybe, God… you might've forgotten a couple of things.**"

I have had many similarly worded conversations and moments of intense prayer with God, like the ones I just described. How about you? If you said yes, then I believe you and I are a lot more like David, than we might have thought.

Even though David had killed Goliath, the Philistines and their army were still *enemy number one* to the people of Israel. David had been a thorn in their side from the moment he stepped onto the battlefield and defeated their champion. And now, captured and in prison, David's life, hangs in the balance, once again!

Can you just imagine, how all of Philistine army must have been reveling and celebrating David's capture? "Oh, great giant killer… What are you going to do now? You're not so big and tough now, are you? You're not so great now, are you? Who are you going to call on now?" **While David was in prison, David's God was not in prison! David's God was still on the throne—as He is today. David's God was able. Our God is still able, still willing, still greatly and worthy to be praised!**

Have you ever felt like you've been in a similar situation? So, what is David to do? What would you have done? I believe David was in the waiting room, which could also be called, *the birthing room*, of his miracle. I don't know about you, but I'd like to think I'd be waiting, while getting my praise on, just like David did!

At this point, David had nowhere to go but to the Lord. David had nowhere else to turn, but to the Lord. Things seemed to be, from the perspective of the outsiders looking in, that David had finally hit the bottom. How many of you know things don't always seem to be the way they appear?

I believe this passage of scripture gives tremendous hope. David's circumstance gives us all hope and courage. Because no matter how many triumphs and accomplishments we read about the "Man after God's own heart", he had times where he was down and he was afraid, just like you and I. Sometimes we forget the low times, and all we remember about David are the amazing stories, the heroic victories, the giants he overcame.

David, after all, was a man. Still flesh and bones like you and me. And, like David, we all get caught up in the moment and we think about our limits. Why is that? It's not like each of us don't already know and aren't aware of our limitations, right? The reality of all our situations always comes back to God's capabilities and God's capabilities alone, even in the crisis, or time of need.

That's why David said, "I'm proud to praise God; fearless now, I trust in God. What can mere mortals do?" Another way of saying it is... "If God be for me,... who can be against me"? **David knew, with God on his side, he was an un-defeat-able army of one!** The devil would like us to think otherwise. He presents our struggle as a one-on-one conflict—him against you alone. The lying accuser knows better than anyone, *if God is for you, friend, it's "game over!" Nothing else matters. Nothing!*

David recognized God's mercy and grace. By David's words he spoke, God recognized David's faith. Did you get that? Let me bring a little bit more clarity to the statement. **David recognized God's mercy. And by David's words he spoke, God recognized David's faith!**

The exact same thing can be said about you, in the spiritual realm of the kingdom of God! Your words, God recognizes as faith, when you are willing to proclaim how much bigger God is than your troubles appear to be!

The Bible declares, over and over, "Your WORDS have power!" Use them wisely! Be sure to use what you're saying to your benefit! Be sure to use and craft your words wisely.

David reminds us all again and declares:

> Psalms 56:12-13 MSG — *GOD IS MIGHTY and TRUE TO HIS WORD! God, you did everything you promised, and I'm thanking you with all my heart. You pulled me from the brink of death, my feet from the cliff-edge of doom. Now I stroll at leisure with God in the sunlit fields of life.*

God had rescued David, and for the rescuing, David was Grateful. David, was offering up his thanks to God for keeping His Promise. **Let me remind you friends, God keeps His Promises and God keeps His Word.**

The truth is, sometimes we need to encourage ourselves by what we have been given, and with God's Faithfulness to us! How God always keeps his promises and keeps His word to us! When we are the ones going through the difficulties of life, when we're down in the valley, thinking we're going through our struggles alone, David reminds us, here in scripture, that nothing could be further from the truth!

Who else would do this for us, but God? Here's the short version of what David was really saying: "I know my enemies are going to be turned back! I know God is going to make me victorious over my enemies! I know God is going to give me victory over my trouble and my trials, because I know GOD IS FOR ME!"

David was leading by example. In summary he was saying:

> ***God is on my side!*** *When it seems like everything that can go wrong is going wrong...* ***God is for me!****. When it seems like nobody cares about what's going on in my life...****God is for me!*** *When the valley is so deep, it seems as though things are never going to bottom out, and the mountain top experience, that was here just a minute ago, is now out of sight!* ***God is still, yes God is still for me and will always and forevermore be for me!***

What words are you saying to encourage yourself when you're going through hard situations? Someone once said, "I know God won't give me anything I can't handle, I just wish He wouldn't trust me with so much!" And yes, sometimes it does *feel* like God trusts us with too much. But we forget we are not alone. The truth is, **God will never give us more than we can handle, or that His grace can't see us through!** When Joseph was in the prison, do you know what gave him hope? When Paul and Silas were shackled and chained, do you know what gave them hope? It was the same thing that gave David hope while in the Philistine prison. It was the fact that if God was for them. Nothing else mattered. ***God is for you! Nothing else matters.***

> Luke 7:22-23 TPT — *Only then did Jesus answer the question posed by John's disciples. "Now go back and tell John what you have just seen and heard here today. The blind are now seeing. The crippled are now walking. Those who were lepers are now cured. Those who were deaf are now hearing. Those who were dead are now brought back to life. The poor and broken are given the hope of salvation. And tell John these words: The blessing of heaven comes upon those who never lose their faith in me, no matter what happens."*

These are Jesus' words to John and to you: ***The blessing of heaven comes upon those who never lose their faith in me, no matter what happens.***

I encourage you to commit that to memory as a *go-to* scripture when you take a stand every time the devil comes against you! Because, problems are going to come. Problems are going to come and go a whole lot quicker for those who never lose their faith in Jesus, no matter what happens!

Now, I don't know about you, child of God. But I'm glad I serve the same great God that David served! I'm glad I know and I have the same Jesus living in my heart—the same Jesus available to all those people who were **healed** of illnesses in Luke chapter 7. The same God who **moved** Joseph from the prison to the palace. The same God who **shook** the prison walls for Paul and Silas. The same God who **delivered** David from the hands of the Philistines! The same God is still just as powerful—still on the throne. He is still just as attentive to you and me, as He was when David wrote this Psalm. Truthfully, if we know that, is there anything else we need to know?

Is there anything else we need to know, if we know God is for us? The answer is *no*. There's really nothing else that we need to know. Does that mean we know it all? I know some of us would probably like to think so. But truly, that my friends, is all we need to know, and I guess if we know that piece of information, then you could say, I suppose we know it all!

But the arguments fill our thoughts: "David was a Bible hero." "David had great courage." "David had great faith." "David was a man after God's own Heart." **Don't you know? David doesn't have anything on you!** God has given us each a personal invitation by His own Son Jesus, and called us to be a child of the King. That's a big deal! There is no bigger deal than that right there, my friend! Some people may try to *one-up* you, but let me tell you, there is no *one-upping* someone who has become a child of the One, true, living God!

The King of England has called different men to be *Royal Knights of England*. Actors have been applauded for their acting skills with an *Oscar*. Musicians have been awarded *Grammys* for songwriting and singing. The *Pulitzer Prize*, the *Nobel Peace Prize* and the list of human achievable accolades goes on and on. I even read the other day, that the last two remaining *Beatles* have a combined net worth of $1.6 billion dollars. That's a huge amount of money. If Billion is too big to imagine, that's 1,600 million dollars. As great of an achievement, and all those other achievements seem to be, they all fail most miserably in comparison with being called, **Child of The King!**

If you are a Child of The King, you should realize and know that God is for you. God has called you to Greatness. Your best days don't lay behind you, your best days are still ahead of you.

Wherever you're at in life—and no matter where you're at in life—it's not yet, "as good as it gets!" There are too many people who have never taken a leisurely stroll with their Maker. Why? Because they're trying to carry all the burdens of life with them. They carry their burden at all times, in all situations, even though they can barely walk under the heavy load, they never change what they're doing. **If you're not at leisure with God, then you're doing more than you need to be doing.** If you recognize yourself in that statement, it's worth reading again!

You might say, "Well, I'm really not concerned about that many things," or, "I'm only a little bit stressed." Even if it's only a little bit of stress, it's still stress, isn't it? You're carrying more than you need to be carrying! **Stop doing what you're doing!**

Maybe there was a time when you were really down and out. Maybe you were really sick. I mean really, really sick and there's nothing that you could do, or anyone else could do either! At that point, you hit bottom and cried out to God and you praised God to heal you! And even though healing wasn't happening, you knew there was no other alternative, and you knew that you couldn't overcome your situation alone! You knew God was your only way out! You were at the point of *nothing else matters!*

In 2020, when I had Covid, at times I didn't know if I would even have another breath to praise God. At one point, I called the hospital and told them what my oxygen level was, and they told me it wasn't bad enough for them to admit me into the hospital. I remember hanging up the phone angrily and thinking to myself, "I'm dying here people, I can't even breathe! What good are you people?" —In that moment, I realized what I already knew.

I wanted *them* to be my source. I was looking for people to be my source. But they weren't my source. They weren't even capable of being my source. God was my source! I wasn't angry at God, but I was sure angry at whatever had caused the illness. I had been praying for healing all along. But, in that moment, I began praying like I should've been praying the entire time. **I praised, I prayed, and I asked God to heal me, as if He was the only one who *could* heal me. And He healed me!**

Far too many people have come out of a situation, just like that, only when they emerged from the situation, they go right back to their own antics and self-effort ways of living. Completely forgetting about what just happened, and how God rescued them. Listen, if you're able to make a conscious decision to praise God with your last breath, don't forget to make the conscious decision to praise God, with everything you've got, when God has healed you. It may not be your last breath, but when you're on auto-breathing—when you're inhaling and exhaling without even thinking about it—don't forget; Praise God!

I've been thinking about making a sign by the front door of the church. The sign would say, "All burdens, problems, circumstances, needs, attitudes, and agendas, check them here. You are about to enter the sanctuary of the one true living God! This is the house of hope and healing, where we believe anything is possible, and God can and will do what He says He can do. If you're worried about the items you checked here, and if you feel compelled to come back and pick them up later, they will still be here! If not, there's no need to worry about what will happen to them. We will send them to the landfill with the rest of the garbage life gives you each and every day."

And the same could be said in each of our lives. At any given moment of any given day, do the same thing. Drop your burdens at the door Monday through Saturday as well. Leave them there!

We need to get used to practicing the unforced rhythms of Grace that God wants to pour out in our lives. We can let go of all our worries, and let God do what He has Promised He will do for us. And we can be at peace with that decision.

Matthew 11:30 NKJV — *For My yoke is easy and My burden is light.*

Have you ever really laid all your burdens down? You know, all your needs, all of your stress, for everyone and everything at Jesus' feet? If you haven't, you should! It's where the *peace that passes all understanding* breathes, lives, and thrives!

The Message says it like this:

> MSG — *Are you tired? Worn out? Burned out on religion? Come to me. Get away with me and you'll recover your life. I'll show you how to take a real rest. Walk with me and work with me— watch how I do it. Learn the unforced rhythms of grace. I won't lay anything heavy or ill-fitting on you. Keep company with me and you'll learn to live freely and lightly.*

No matter what you may be facing, Friends, God wants you to know it's only temporary. Why not simply try resting in His ability from here on out, instead of your own? Trust Him and know that He is all you need to know! If God is for me… **nothing else matters!**

CHAPTER 13

YOU CAN BE FREE

> John 10:10-11 NKJV — *The thief does not come except to steal, and to kill, and to destroy. I have come that they may have life, and that they may have it more abundantly.*

Did you notice, this passage appears in chapters 5 and 11 of this book as well? We live in the day and age where we're constantly reminded the accuser is pulling out all the stops. Truth is, I believe past strategies of the accuser have been elevated to drastically new and historical levels, as we edge closer to the coming of the Son of Man. In one breath, I would like to say that everything the devil wants to use against the church has already been exposed. In the next breath, the little wisdom I have, says, we haven't seen anything yet! But I also say, *greater is He that is in me, than he who is in the world.*

Everything the deceiver does now, is not behind closed doors. It isn't under cover of night anymore. But boastfully he acts, extremely loud and in the open for everyone to see! As blatant as it is, everyone is becoming numb to the severity of what the world calls *the new normal*. When are we going to take a stand and stop making any agreement with any kind of narrative the devil's propaganda machine comes up with?

As I said earlier, thankfully, there has been a shift in the atmosphere of this spiritual battle for the soul of humanity. But the fight is not over. Friends, we must press on and heed the overlooked assignments, which have been neglected for far too long and by too many!

I believe many Christians will think this doesn't need to be said, but I want to bring clarity to the table and to all who are hearing this word. The devil has never wavered one time from his obsession to inflict as much destruction as can on society, turning hearts away from God, and taking as many souls to hell with him as possible.

It's time the body of Christ, took an equally firm stance of resistance and stood in unity. **It's high time that every one of God's Children united together, setting aside religious denominations,** locking arms as one huge army of believers and making the stand to say, "***Enough!***"

Far too many Christians have been in denial for too long about the accuser's methods of attack. The cold, hard truth is, ever so cleverly, the devil has always been using an all out assault against morality and humanity. Little by little, day by day, sometimes moment by moment we have witnessed, and been forced to accept the decay of our basic freedoms and what appears to be society's inability to read a moral compass!

If you don't agree, I would ask you how many more times do we have to witness the death of lives right before our eyes? *Steal, kill, and destroy* with Meth and every other drug and scenario under the sun! So much infighting with each other and so many lies. There is so much deceit on display and kept in secret. What we are witnessing in real time, is a 360 degree attack and assault on the power of the Love of God, and all it stands for—it's an attack from every side, from below, and even from above

> 1 John 4:8 NKJV — *He who does not love does not know God, for God is love.*

The time has come to set aside what we think is our own understanding, our individual interpretation of the Love of God. Instead, we need to band together, like never before, and stick it to the devil, in the only way that will get his attention. Let's completely and intentionally energize all who profess a relationship with Jesus into seeking God on a whole new level, and bring understanding, growth, and unity, to God's people like we never have before!

We have all, I believe, witnessed a great and decisive move of God, with what happened politically in 2024. But I will tell you, do not quit the pursuit of God's covenant of Grace, submitting to God's hand of rule and blessing on our nation.

Still, the spiritual war of flesh and blood rages on around the world, regardless of political or physical victories we all witness. Though the battle rages on, it's not too late to cry out in one voice of unity for God's Love, power and willingness to rescue and defend us and to crush the enemy's plans completely.

Right now, we are in the eye of the hurricane, Even though the heinous things and the relentless attacks by the accuser seem to have quieted down, I must remind you that the enemy's plan to continue attacking Christians hasn't stopped and will never stop until Jesus returns!

While the minions of the devil seem to be confused and in full chaos at the moment, **don't think for a second that the accuser is not quietly and cleverly retooling his machine to kill, steal and destroy,** as well as making new strategies and plans for attack. There has never been a greater time to continue the pursuit of, what Jesus said, were the two greatest commandments ever spoken.

> Matthew 22: 37-40 MSG — *Jesus said, "'Love the Lord your God with all your passion and prayer and intelligence.' This is the most important, the first on any list. But there is a second to set alongside it: 'Love others as well as you love yourself.'*

These two commands are the anchors; everything in God's Law and the Prophets hangs from them. Many say, "Look to the church," because they have heard this plea before. But I say, "What Church?" The Church at best is a diminished version of itself, or what it was even 20 years ago. Many prayer warriors have gone on to their rewards. So, while the church may sound like the answer to our dilemma—and don't get me wrong, the church is vitally necessary—it's so much more than religion that we need in this final hour. We are facing an all out attack on humanity. Bricks and mortar, four walls and a roof, four songs and a sermon, will not rebuke the onslaught of the devil that we are already seeing as a society.

Only faith in God—a personal relationship with Jesus Christ, God's Son—can save us from the destruction and pursuit of the enemy that we see all around us. Religion by itself is empty. Now, don't misunderstand me here; I love the church! But I despise religion, and you should too.

Religion is nothing but man's attempt at making rules and regulations on how to follow and have a relationship with God. Religion is not a relationship. **Religion can't, won't, and doesn't Love God.**

Only a relationship with Jesus offers love for God and the promises of God's Love. Love for God and love for your neighbor is what Jesus said were the greatest commandments. Not the love of self, which is what we have seen lately on the 24/7 daily news cycle. Love of self is promoted at every level. Sadly, it's also what we witness in someone's life who refuses the message of salvation and a relationship with Jesus.

> Eph. 4:6 NKJV — *One God and Father of all, who is above all, and through all, and in you all.*

God is the one who makes all things possible, for in him all things were created. And the love, grace and forgiveness of God, is the only thing that makes all things possible in our lives!

Jesus was very clear, He didn't mix any words about what we were to do, and how we were to act towards one another!

> Mark 10:27 MSG — *Jesus was blunt: "No chance at all if you think you can pull it off by yourself. Every chance in the world if you let God do it."*

Love for God and the Amazing Love of God, is what makes all things possible. Nothing else. Not money, not sex, not drugs, not power, **only love for God, and the amazing Love of God, makes all things possible!** Now is when the Amen corner should be shouting. Friend, if you're not shouting right now, are you sure you are a member of the Amen corner?

Let me make a suggestion to you, friend. Don't be caught standing on the corner of "This isn't the way we do things at my church!" Jump, that's right, I said *jump*! Leap away, from religions' insistence, "This is the way things have always been." Instead, get on board with the new charge of what Jesus wants to do through the relationship you claim to have with Him.

The way of Salvation message was delivered by Jesus through the victory of the cross. The blessing and favor that God wants to place on your life and his love for you, will move you light years ahead of others around you. It will elevate you to positions only God Himself could have gotten you to.

What will be the first thing the accuser tries to do, when you get there? He will do the same thing he has done since the beginning, child of God. You're not above reproach, but his plan is your demise. That's right, **same old, same old, *take you out, and tear you down* plan.** Everything the accuser does, revolves predictably around stealing, killing and destroying anything good or worthwhile.

Satan is relentless, but sly. His tactics are always sugar-coated. They may have a good looking delivery, a pretty face, an attractive smile, or a shiny new paint job, but they still all have one objective. That is, to kill you, to steal from you, to completely destroy you and everyone and everything important to you.

Who doesn't love to hear how great they are? We all do. It's pretty hard to ignore because it's continually craved by our human nature. Who doesn't want to go along with the crowd, when they think everyone is with them and for them? Sometimes it takes restraint not to want to go along with the crowd. No one should ever underestimate the craftiness of the accuser, especially when we see what's happening around the world today!

Some may still choose to accept and go along with what they see because of political pressure, or fear and consequences! These are tricks of the enemy, designed to aid with society's destruction!

One thing is always true, and the truth will always set you free. Here is the absolute truth; "When you have a love for God and the love of God is in you, there is nothing to fear! God's love always casteth out fear!" This is not just some of the time, but forever, always, every time, and without fail! The Bible tells us, *Absolutely nothing can come between you and the love of God!* I know this seems redundant, but I want you to hear yourself say it out loud; "Nothing, nothing, nothing can come between me and the love that God has for me!"

> Romans 8:38-39 NLT — *I am convinced that nothing can ever separate us from God's love. Neither death nor life, neither angels nor demons, neither our fears for today nor our worries about tomorrow— not even the powers of hell can separate us from God's love. 39 No power in the sky above or in the earth below—indeed, nothing in all creation will ever be able to separate us from the love of God that is revealed in Christ Jesus our Lord.*

When you need deliverance, when you need a miracle, it's not enough to *know about* the One True God. When you need an answer to a problem, you need to **know God!** When you need your peace of mind, while you're going through a mountainous situation, **when things are beyond your control—if you're honest, this is every waking minute of your life—you need to know God!**

Everyone needs to know the One True Living God in a personal way, in a close personal relationship.

Your mama's faith, your daddy's faith, nobody else's relationship with Jesus, will automatically bring you peace, comfort and the miracles you are desiring to meet your needs in your life!

You must find and build your own personal connection, your own personal pathway to the relationship of love only Jesus can offer! You need to have your own personal relationship with Jesus, God's only begotten Son, the Savior of the world, who willingly laid down his own life and was crucified on the cross. He was crucified for your sin. Willingly, he paid your ransom for your freedom and eternal destiny. God always offers hope. Even when you don't know Jesus personally; Even when the accuser tries to convince you otherwise, God still offers you immense and unlimited hope! It's something the accuser truly can never offer!

Every story we read of our Bible heroes, David, Moses, Joshua, Ruth and all the way to Mathew, Mark, Paul and John, each had a relationship with God. They believed in what they had, stepped out in faith, and refused to bow down to the accuser. And what happened to them every time? The peace of God, *peace which passes all understanding,* came and flooded their spirit, even while Jesus made the impossible become possible, for each of them!

The most amazing thing, still to this day, is that **God stands ready to do the same, for whoever is willing to put their faith and trust in Jesus**—in His forgiveness, in His salvation, in His Love, willingness and never ending abilities.

Peter gave us clear instructions and a stern reminder, to never forget what is possible.

> 1st Peter 5:8-11 MSG — *Keep a cool head. Stay alert. The Devil is poised to pounce, and would like nothing better than to catch you napping. Keep your guard up. You're not the only ones plunged into these hard times. It's the same with Christians all over the world. So keep a firm grip on the faith. The suffering won't last forever. It won't be long before this generous God who has great plans for us in Christ— eternal and glorious plans they are!— will have you put together and on your feet for good. He gets the last word; yes, he does. God always has the first word, the last word, and every other word on everything in between!*

Praise God! This is a word you can trust for everything and even trust with your life. The world and the condemning report of the enemy, continues to try and tell us things are bleak, harder times are yet to come, our darkest hour has yet to arrive.

The devil's henchmen and women are always poised to pounce. Their message will always try to convince and give the report that we will find ourselves in the lion's den, or so it seems.

Now is *not the time* to give in to the roar of the lions. Now is the time to trust the report of the Lord! It's time to trust the thunderous explosion of the Holy Ghost (God on earth) power, being released in Heaven and about to sweep the earth, bringing an awakening of revival, and demanding justice!

It's time for amazing Justice for every praying, born again, faith-wielding, child of the most High God! Not only for justice, but also retribution for everything ever stolen, or taken away from God's people. All for this purpose: The amazing redistribution of such property, with the heavy favor of God's multiplied interest of retribution. It's something that only God can deliver.

There is a great move of God on the horizon! Thank you, Lord for the coming Revival. Friends, I have confidence to tell you, it's coming! Our best days are not behind us, our best days have already been determined and are quickly coming. We must be prepared. **These are the good ole days we are going to look back and remember warmly.**

Embrace these days with anticipation! Let our prayer be:

> *Great God and Loving ABBA, Father,*
> *let Your plans become our destiny!*
> *Let me be a part of your plan, Lord!*
> *Let my lips be Your lips!*
> *Let my hands be your hands,*
> *let my feet be Your feet.*
> *And let Your will become every believer's will and prayer!*

I want to ask one more time, if you're still reading. Have you personally experienced the Power of the Holy Spirit? The Spirit that God sent after His son Jesus came to earth, and died on the cross, to deliver?

Maybe you're still thinking and reading along, still waiting to make a decision,… thinking to yourself, "will this *infilling of the Holy Spirit* really change my life and the relationship I already have with Jesus?" And I can tell you, undoubtedly, a thousand times, "Yes, it will!" It changed my life, and I know it will change your life and relationship with Jesus in extraordinary ways—beyond what you can think or imagine!

Don't you think it's time you did? I think you already know the answer. All you have to do is ask God to fill you with His life changing and liberating gift and infilling of His Holy Spirit. And God will. He said He will, and He will. You will never be the same.

Isn't it time to *Run Towards the Light*, like you never have before? Isn't it time to get more busy than you've been at any moment in your entire life?

> *The bad news is, time flies.*
> *The good news is, you're the pilot.*
> — Michael Altshuler

Time is so short, friends. If not now, will you ever commit to run the race to win, and not take your eyes off the prize of Jesus! Not only the prize of your eternity, but the eternity of everyone you come in contact with who needs Jesus along the way!

CHAPTER 14

ACCOUNTABILITY STARTS TODAY

I think all Christians would agree, because we have witnessed the event. We live in this moment of time, for such a time as this! It's no coincidence that the whole world has become numb to the severity of what today is called *the new normal*. And it's no coincidence we are alive today, and we have been called by Jesus, to *change the narrative*. The narrative is changing, one life story at a time.

We must continue to stand united, each doing our part. Helping to remove the dark cloud of oppression and to bring the much needed change to the spiritual atmosphere. In a world that has been, for far too long, running away from, instead of towards, the Light of Jesus, and the common sense Gospel message!

As I watched the changing of the guard of the free world, this morning January 20, 2025, optimism and relief seemed to be darting on every side of the spectrum. As the new sheriff in town, he both accepted his position and announced his long awaited arrival of Hope! Greater optimism, I believe, was acknowledged, when the real hero of our world, was credited by what was done. When the new sheriff's life had been spared earlier this year, twice from assassination attempts.

Make no mistake, while we may not see Jesus coming in the clouds, Jesus is not far from the amazing event taking place! And while we admire one man who seemingly has done the impossible, with the blessing and protection of God in his life, the real hero's going forward, from the story of the day, will be the men and women, who arise to the recurring task, which Jesus presented to His children! The original challenge, to reach all of the world—until the whole world knows—with the message of the Gospel. If you're still with me, reading up till now, that's no mistake either! Being alive in 2025, in this critical era in the history of Christianity. Whether you accept the call to arms and enter the most important fight of your life with Jesus—standing against the principalities of darkness—or not, is irrelevant! You have been called, and one day, will be held accountable. What did you do with your calling?

Today, the question is, "What will you do with it?" What have you done with your calling of relationship and discipleship so far? This is not simply a new era in politics, and a time of prosperity. I believe this will begin the era of the greatest outpouring of the Holy Spirit and harvest of souls for the Kingdom of Heaven that we have ever witnessed!

I hope, somehow, that this book, by the divine inspiration of the Holy Spirit, will inspire you to pursue in a new and refreshing way, to pursue your calling like you never have before.

Truthfully, nothing I've written is new, and I don't want to claim any credit. I would relate to you though, some of the most inspired times in and throughout my life were the reconnection with the basic things I knew to do, but somehow had forgotten. I had been neglecting them for far too long. The point is, **this is decision time!** Maybe you've been here before, standing at this same crossroad, with uncertainty clouding your mind.

Nonetheless, I challenge you to get on board with the plans of God that He has for your life. There is so much work to be done, yet, the laborers are so few in number. Yet Jesus said, "the harvest is and will truly be, one of momentous proportions!"

Will you help and do your part? Will you be like Isaiah?

> Isaiah 6:8 NIV — *Then I heard the voice of the Lord saying, "Whom shall I send? And who will go for us?" And I said, "Here am I. Send me!"*

I hope you will! I hope you will accept the challenge and *Run Towards the Light*, with a new and refreshed vigor. Run like you never have before!

The choice is yours, my friend! For me, it's an easy choice. The accuser will tell you, however, it's a tough choice. Don't listen to him. **Don't make one more agreement with any thought of you doing anything but what God is calling you to!**

This is not the end, my friend, this is only the beginning of the next chapter of your own story, living the amazing opportunity and life you have been given. It's your story within Jesus' amazing story! The humble beginning of something that will be celebrated for all of eternity!

I pray and hope the absolute best that God has to offer, will come flooding into your relationship, into your understanding and into your very soul. And that Jesus will guide you safely, all the way to eternity and the Victor's Circle! As you ***Run Towards the Light!***

MEET THE AUTHOR

Charlie has been identified by several different career choices throughout his life. If you ask his most important calling, and identity-of-choice, he will say, "Grace believing, faith and Spirit filled, intimate friend, devoted follower and son of the Most High God! I made a lot of decisions in life like a lot of people, the best decision I made was to let my relationship with Jesus change my life!"

When asked why he became a writer, Charlie says, "I want everyone to have at least equal opportunity to have the amazing relationship that I have with the Lord, and hopefully an even better one!" Ultimately, wanting to tell as many people about Jesus and take as many souls to heaven with him as possible is Charlie's mission.

Charlie is also happily married to his amazing wife, Cindy. They have three children and four grandchildren. Together they are co-pastors of *Calvary Temple,* "God's House of Hope and Healing", in Monticello, Indiana. They love to minister, travel, share their Love of Jesus, and the love they have for each other, with everyone they meet.

If you have never asked Jesus into your heart, I encourage you to read through these few steps and scriptures. God loves you. Jesus died for you. And the Holy Spirit of God is ready to come teach you, comfort you, to help you become the man or woman God is calling you to be!

The *Romans Road* is a simple series of Bible verses that outline the path to salvation:

> Step #1: *All have sinned and fall short of the Glory of God.* [Romans 3:23]
>
> Step #2: *Sin entered the world through one man, and death through sin.* [Romans 5:12]
>
> Step #3: *God demonstrates his own love for us in this: While we were still sinners, Christ died for us.* [Romans 5:8]
>
> Step #4: *The wages of sin is death, but the gift of God is eternal life in Christ Jesus our Lord.* [Romans 6:23]

Step #5: *If you declare with your mouth, "Jesus is Lord," and believe in your heart that God raised him from the dead, you will be saved.* [Romans 10:9-10]

Visit **parkinglotfaith.com** for the latest news and links to more books you will enjoy by Charlie Roberts:
* *I Am, I Can, I Will*
* *My Scandalous Relationship With God*
* *Parking Lot Faith*
* *One Moment Of Faith Changes Everything*
* *He Knows My Name,* a modern musical

Available on amazon.com — Author copies are also available for teaching and group study.

A PERSONAL NOTE FROM CHARLIE

If you don't know Jesus personally, now is the time! Please, pray this with me;

Jesus, I know that I'm a sinner. I believe that you died and rose again for me, please come into my heart and be my Lord and Savior! Thank you for saving me and giving me eternal life!

Friend, if that was you, I encourage you to get into a Bible believing church that preaches believes in faith and everything we've covered—all that Jesus went to the Cross to give you!

The Bible also says to share what you've done with someone, and let them know that you are a Christian who has been born again! I welcome hearing from you, especially if you don't have anyone else to share that news with—share it with me!

I will be more than happy to welcome you into the Family of God!

Charlie Roberts

Email Charlie Roberts: keeper47960@yahoo.com

www.ingramcontent.com/pod-product-compliance
Lightning Source LLC
Chambersburg PA
CBHW072009090426
42734CB00033B/2136